Unhittable

Reliving the Magic and
Drama of Baseball's
Best-Pitched Games

James Buckley Jr.
and Phil Pepe

TRIUMPH
BOOKS

CHICAGO

Produced in partnership and licensed by Major League Baseball Properties, Inc.
Vice President of Publishing, Don Hintze

Library of Congress Cataloging-in-Publication Data

Buckley, James, 1963–
    Unhittable, reliving the magic and drama of baseball's best-pitched games / James Buckley, Jr. and Phil Pepe.
        p. cm.
    Includes index.
    ISBN 1-57243-666-2
    1. Pitching (Baseball)—United States—History. 2. Pitchers (Baseball)—United States—Biography. I. Pepe, Phil. II. Title.

    GV871.B77 2004
    796.357'22—dc22

                                                                        2004051646

Parts of this book are based on material previously published in *Perfect: The Inside Story of Baseball's Sixteen Perfect Game*s by James Buckley Jr., published by Triumph Books in 2002.

This book is available in quantity at special discounts for your group or organization. For further information, contact:

Triumph Books
601 South LaSalle Street
Suite 500
Chicago, Illinois 60605
(312) 939-3330
Fax (312) 663-3557

Printed in U.S.A.
ISBN 1-57243-666-2
Design by Ray Ramos; page design by Jason Hinman/Mojo Media.

Contents

Foreword

One of the side benefits of pitching in the major leagues for 27 years was that I got to see some of the greatest pitchers in the history of the game up close and personal—including the one I consider the most dominant, overpowering pitcher I have ever seen: Sandy Koufax.

I had seen Sandy pitch several times on television, and I could hardly believe my eyes, he was so great. Then, when I came up to the Mets late in the 1966 season, I had the pleasure of seeing him in person, and he was just as unbelievable. It turned out that was his last season in the major leagues. He retired soon after because of arthritis, but the way he pitched, you would never have believed he wasn't 100 percent. He won 27 games, had an ERA of 1.73, struck out 317, had 27 complete games, five shutouts, and a no-hitter. What a great loss it was when he left the game!

I've seen Bob Feller, Warren Spahn, and Robin Roberts on film, but never in person. And I have never even seen films of the greats of the distant past, like Walter Johnson, Cy Young, Christy Mathewson, Lefty Grove, and Carl Hubbell; however, I have read about them, studied their stats, and I have nothing but admiration for what these men achieved. But I firmly believe that the pitchers of my era, especially those in the sixties and seventies, were as good as any who ever played the game.

Right behind Koufax I put Bob Gibson; my good friend and former team-mate Tom Seaver; Juan Marichal; and Steve Carlton. Those are the guys I liked to watch pitch. I also enjoyed watching Ron Guidry. For his size, his intensity and the stuff he had were amazing. Among recent pitchers, I'd put Randy Johnson and my fellow Texan, Roger Clemens, right up there with the best.

The game of baseball hasn't changed a great deal over the past 100 years, but the philosophy of pitching certainly has, and I'm sad to say that I don't like what has transpired with pitch counts and the use of relief pitchers, long men, set-up men, and closers. The mindset of today's pitchers is totally different than it was in the past. Today's pitchers don't seem to look at it as their game. It used to be that this was your game, your start, and you wanted to be there at the end.

Maybe that's not the pitchers' fault. Maybe it's the fault of the people who seem to be running the game with computers. They have programmed young pitchers to have a different mindset. Today they don't call their own games, and they go out with the thought that if they give their team five good innings, they've done their job. By the sixth inning, they're looking over their shoulder to see who's warming up in the bullpen.

The concept of pitching has evolved over the different eras, and as time went on, the pitcher was asked to do less and less. In the early days, pitchers—the good ones—would start every third day. Then it became every fourth day. In the forties and fifties, they would start and relieve between starts. Then they went to the five-man rotation. Now, they only start every fifth day, and when they reach 100 pitches, they're out of there. My observation is that things started to change when the home run became more prevalent.

One thing that hasn't changed in baseball over the past 100 years is the importance of pitching. It's still the most vital part of the game—always was, always will be. Nothing happens in a game until the pitcher releases the ball. The fate of his team is in his hand. You don't win if you don't pitch well. How many times have you heard it, and in how many different ways? It was true in Cy Young's day, it's true today, and it will be true 100 years from today.

For that reason, I welcome this book, *Unhittable: Reliving the Magic and Drama of Baseball's Best-Pitched Games*, because it's completely devoted to pitching: the great careers, the great seasons, the great games, and the greatest pitchers in the history of baseball.

Speaking for the pitching fraternity and for everyone who ever stood 60'6" away from a major league hitter, I'm grateful for the attention.

–Nolan Ryan

PART I

The Early Modern Era

Pre-1900 to 1945

Ralph Kiner's Top 20 Pitchers of All Time

1. Bob Feller
2. Warren Spahn
3. Walter Johnson
4. Grover Cleveland Alexander
5. Sandy Koufax
6. Lefty Grove
7. Tom Seaver
8. Christy Mathewson
9. Nolan Ryan
10. Steve Carlton
11. Bob Gibson
12. Dizzy Dean
13. Robin Roberts
14. Randy Johnson
15. Jim Palmer
16. Juan Marichal
17. Cy Young
18. Carl Hubbell
19. Roger Clemens
20. Ewell Blackwell

Ernie Harwell's Top 20 Pitchers of All Time

1. Cy Young
2. Christy Mathewson
3. Warren Spahn
4. Walter Johnson
5. Nolan Ryan
6. Randy Johnson
7. Steve Carlton
8. Bob Gibson
9. Hoyt Wilhelm
10. Lefty Grove
11. Bob Feller
12. Grover Cleveland Alexander
13. Curt Schilling
14. Sandy Koufax
15. Mickey Lolich
16. Whitey Ford
17. Tom Seaver
18. Ed Walsh
19. Greg Maddux
20. Phil Niekro

Founding Fathers

It was with awe and wonderment that fans left St. Louis' Sportsman's Park on the afternoon of July 15, 1876. They could barely hide their astonishment or control their excitement. Not only had they just watched their hometown baseball team, the St. Louis Brown Stockings in the newly formed National League, defeat the Hartford Dark Blues by the score of 2–0, but they had witnessed something extraordinary, something unthinkable.

Pitching for the Brown Stockings, George Washington Bradley, nicknamed "Grin" because he had a perpetual grin on his face, had completed nine full innings and had not allowed a single safe hit.

The fledgling National League, formed the year Alexander Graham Bell invented the telephone, was not yet three months old, but the ecstatic St. Louis rooters knew they had been witnesses to baseball history.

Word spread rapidly to the other cities in the embryonic baseball league, and for days in Philadelphia, Boston, Louisville, New York, Cincinnati, Hartford, and Chicago, everyone talked about the wondrous St. Louis happening. When the first season ended without another pitcher matching the accomplishment, it was agreed that Bradley's feat had been an aberration, one that was not likely to happen ever again.

George Washington Bradley is generally regarded as "the father of the no-hitter," but there must be a place for Joseph Borden.

Poor Joe Borden. History dealt him a cruel blow, for it was Joseph Emley Borden, also known as Joseph Emley Josephs, who threw the first recorded no-hitter on July 28, 1875, when he defeated Chicago 4–0 while pitching for Philadelphia of the National Association. But that was in the dark ages of the sport. Bradley's no-hitter stands as the first because it was achieved in the National League's inaugural season.

However, Hall of Fame historian Lee Allen uncovered facts to prove that Borden actually beat Bradley to the no-hitter by two months in 1876, but the game was not recognized.

According to Allen, Borden pitched the National League's first no-hitter for Boston on May 23, 1876, in an 8–0 victory over Cincinnati. The reason it was not recognized is that the box score shows two hits in the game for Cincinnati. Allen explained the mix-up in his book *100 Years of Baseball*, published in 1950:

Although the game was played in Boston, the score was sent to the league office by Oliver Perry Caylor, a writer for The Cincinnati Enquirer, *and during the season Caylor, at variance with contemporary scorers, counted bases on*

balls as hits. Later, in 1887, bases on balls were to count as hits, but in the league's first campaign only Caylor scored them as such. Borden granted to two Cincinnati batters passes which appeared as hits in the box score.

The box score in question showed another characteristic of the times: 20 errors were made in the game, but 9 of them were charged to catchers because passed balls in 1876 were charged as errors. Two other errors were charged to Borden because wild pitches also were scored as errors.

In 1876 fielding was not the highly developed skill it is now. Gloves were still not in use, and catchers played behind the batter only when there were runners on base.

After his two "no-hitters," poor Joe Borden fell on the kind of hard times that typified his unhappy fate as a player, and he slipped into a shadowy past. He suffered a sore arm later that season and finished out the year as groundskeeper of the Boston ballpark. A few years later he turned up in a Philadelphia factory stitching baseballs like those he once threw past opposing batters.

In 1876 pitchers stood 45 feet from the batter and threw the ball underhanded, softball-style. With his team playing just two or three times a week, and a much less rigorous style of pitching, George Washington Bradley was a one-man pitching rotation for the St. Louis Brown Stockings. They played 64 games in the season, and Bradley was the starting pitcher for all 64. He won 45 and lost 19, and his St. Louis team finished second to the Chicago White Stockings.

Bradley's no-hitter was the third game of a three-game series with Hartford. Bradley not only started all three games, he pitched three consecutive shutouts and finished the season with 16 shutouts, a record that stood until it was tied by Grover Cleveland Alexander 40 years later.

But Bradley was never to approach the success he had in his first season. He played nine more years, with a record of only 93–108. Never again would he hold the opponent's batters without a hit. And he would spend most of his remaining playing days as a third baseman.

For nearly four years after Bradley's 1876 no-hitter, no pitcher could match the feat, reinforcing the original belief that baseball would never see another such performance of pitching perfection. But when Lawrence J. Corcoran of Chicago and James Galvin of Buffalo pitched no-hitters on consecutive days in August of 1880, the baseball lawmakers decided the pitcher had gained too great an advantage over the hitter, and they voted to move the pitching rubber from 45 feet to 50 feet from home plate. Apparently, the desired result was achieved because there was no no-hitter thrown in 1881.

It wasn't long before pitchers regained their advantage over hitters, and in 1882, with a second league—the American Association—in oper-

Bradley pictured with his ballclub, the St. Louis Brown Stockings.

ation, there were three no-hitters, including a second one by Corcoran, who proved that pitching distance made little difference to him. Two years later, Corcoran, a native of Brooklyn, New York, became the first pitcher to throw three no-hitters, a record that would be tied twice, but not surpassed until 81 years later by another Brooklynite, Sandy Koufax.

With three no-hitters pitched in the 1891 and 1892 seasons, once again the baseball lords decided to change the pitching distance, this time to 60 feet, six inches, where it has remained to this day. Again the move had the desired effect, as there was just one no-hitter pitched in 1893 and none in the next three seasons.

In the six years from 1914 to 1919, there were 22 no-hitters (including 5 in the Federal League) with a peak of 6 in 1917, the most ever pitched in any year during the modern era. In 1920, the lawmakers went to work again to legislate against the pitcher and banned the spitball, not only to take away an effective weapon for the pitcher, but for sanitary and safety reasons as well. In the six years following the spitball ban, only seven no-hitters were pitched.

Once again, pitchers being an inventive and constantly improving lot, there were 12 no-hitters pitched in the 13 years from 1929 to 1941. Following World War II, pitchers broke out with a rash of no-hitters—15 in the first seven postwar years.

It is interesting to note that despite the advent of the lively ball, during a period when home run totals escalated, the number of no-hitters increased rather than decreased. In the eight-year period from 1960 to 1967, there were 23 no-hitters in both major leagues. From 1960 until 1982, there was at least one no-hitter pitched in every major league season, an indication that there will be no end to what George Washington Bradley—or Joseph Emley Borden—started more than a century and a quarter ago.

G. W. BRADLEY'S NO-HITTER
JULY 15, 1876

St. Louis	AB	R	H	RBI
Cuthbert, lf	NA	1	0	NA
Clapp, c	-	0	3	-
McGeary, 2b	-	0	0	-
Pike, cf	-	0	1	-
Battin, 3b	-	0	0	-
Blong, rf	-	1	1	-
Bradley, p	-	0	1	-
Dehlman, 1b	-	0	1	-
Pearce, ss	-	0	1	-
Totals	-	**2**	**8**	-

Hartford	AB	R	H	RBI
Remsen, cf	NA	0	0	NA
Burdock, 2b	-	0	0	-
Higham, rf	-	0	0	-
Ferguson, 3b	-	0	0	-
Carey, ss	-	0	0	-
Bond, p	-	0	0	-
York, lf	-	0	0	-
Mills, 1b	-	0	0	-
Harbidge, c	-	0	0	-
Totals	-	**0**	**0**	-

	1	2	3	4	5	6	7	8	9	R	H	E
StL	1	1	0	0	0	0	0	0	0	2	8	3
Har	0	0	0	0	0	0	0	0	0	0	0	4

St. Louis	IP	H	R	ER	BB	K
George Bradley (W)	9	0	0	0	1	NA

Hartford	IP	H	R	ER	BB	K
Tommy Bond (L)	9	8	2	0	0	NA

Time—2:00

Bradley is widely recognized as the "father of the no-hitter."

Borden beat Bradley to the feat, but not to the record books.

John Lee Richmond
Perfect Game
June 12, 1880

John M. Ward
Perfect Game
June 17, 1880

A Perfect Week for Baseball

While George Bradley was the "founder" of the no-hitter, it would be an unsung rookie lefty who "created" the perfect game. However, although John Lee Richmond of the late and lamented Worcester, Massachusetts, Brown Stockings faced only 27 members of the opposing Cleveland Forest Citys, his feat would not be called "perfect" for 42 more years. But perfect it was.

Amazingly, only five days later, future Hall of Famer John M. Ward pitched the second perfect game. Baseball had been a pro sport for nine years, and these were the first perfect games. It would be another 24 years before anyone threw another. This is just one of those amazing statistical coincidences that make baseball so much fun.

But first to John Lee Richmond. Unlike many players of the day, he was a college man, a successful student at Brown University (he would go on to become a teacher and much-admired school administrator in his native Toledo, Ohio, where a cemetery marker celebrates his place in baseball history). In fact, he had led his team to the 1879 national collegiate baseball title over Yale. After that season he played for what was then the semipro Worcester Brown Stockings (although whether that was their official nickname is debated), tossing a seven-inning no-hitter in an exhibition against the professional Chicago White Stockings.

By 1880 he was officially a pro, but waited until the end of the school year to join the team. That end came on June 11 with an all-night college party called "Class Day." The early morning wrap-up of the celebration was actually a baseball game that Richmond pitched. It started at 5:00 A.M. on June 12 and wrapped up about 6:30.

After a few hours of what can only be assumed to be less-than-restful sleep, Richmond was on a train to Providence to pitch—for the second time that day—for Worcester.

Richmond employed a surprising variety of pitches. He even had a breaking ball that so baffled Brown science teachers that he performed a demonstration for them to prove that indeed "a pitched sphere might change its horizontal course during a pitch and that the 'curve' was not an optical illusion." He was also one of only two left-handers pitching regularly in what was then the sole "big league."

The key to the game, contemporary scribes felt, was not Richmond, but the team's defense. A game without an error was nearly unheard of in a time with lumpy baseballs, choppy fields, and players with no gloves.

Richmond had no trouble in the early going, with his catcher Charley Bennett (later the namesake of the home field of the Tigers, which was Bennett Park from 1901 to 1912) helping out by nabbing two "foul bounds" (see sidebar pg. 7). But in the fifth came a play that remains unique in the history of perfect games. Cleveland first baseman Bill Phillips led off that inning with a hard shot to right. Worcester's right fielder, Alonzo Knight, charged the ball, fielded it on one hop, and, without stopping, fired a strike to first. Umpire "Foghorn" Bradley, the game's sole arbiter, called Phillips out.

In the bottom of that inning, Worcester got a gift when Fred Dunlap committed two errors on one play, allowing Worcester's Arthur Irwin to score the game's only run.

The game was interrupted briefly by a rainstorm in the seventh, but the delay didn't bother Richmond a bit. He "did some lively work" with the sawdust sprinkled on the pitcher's box (meaning that the *Worcester Daily* writer thought that Richmond might have been adding a bit to the ball).

And so, two innings later, it quickly ended, unremarkably. Richmond and his teammates had put together history's first perfect game.

The key to the game, contemporary scribes felt, was not Richmond, but the team's defense. A game without an error was nearly unheard of in a time with lumpy baseballs, choppy fields, and players with no gloves (though some catchers wore leather palm pads). "Richmond was most effectively supported," wrote one paper. "Every position on the home nine being played to perfection." A *Chicago Tribune* article called it "the most wonderful game on record," yet failed to mention who had pitched the game!

As the history of perfect games and other unhittable events went forward, Richmond was often contacted for his thoughts. In a 1910 interview, he said, "Pitching such a game 30 years ago didn't make the same sensation [it would today]. I don't recall that any particular fuss was made about it by any newspaper or set of fans."

If Richmond's feat earned little acclaim at the time, John M. Ward's perfecto, coming five days later, is like the silver medalist in the 100 meters—no one remembers who finished second. However, Ward is one of the few perfect-game pitchers who would have been baseball immortals even had lightning not struck them for one special day.

JOHN LEE RICHMOND'S PERFECT GAME
JUNE 12, 1880

Cleveland	AB	R	H	RBI
Dunlap, 2b	3	0	0	NA
Hankinson, 3b	3	0	0	-
Kennedy, c	3	0	0	-
Phillips, 1b	3	0	0	-
Shaffer, rf	3	0	0	-
McCormick, p	3	0	0	-
Gilligan, cf	3	0	0	-
Glasscock, ss	3	0	0	-
Hanlon, lf	3	0	0	-
Totals	27	0	0	-

Worcester	AB	R	H	RBI
Wood, lf	4	0	0	NA
Richmond, p	3	0	1	-
Knight, rf	3	0	0	-
Irwin, ss	3	1	2	-
Bennett, c	2	0	0	-
Whitney, 3b	3	0	0	-
Sullivan, 1b	3	0	0	-
Corey, cf	3	0	0	-
Creamer, 2b	3	0	0	-
Totals	27	1	3	-

	1	2	3	4	5	6	7	8	9	R	H	E
Cle	0	0	0	0	0	0	0	0	0	0	0	2
Wor	0	0	0	0	1	0	0	0	x	1	3	0

Cleveland	IP	H	R	ER	BB	K
McCormick (L)	8.0	3	1	-	1	7

Worcester	IP	H	R	ER	BB	K
Richmond (W)	9.0	0	0	0	0	5

Time—1:26

Richmond (top) was the author of the first-known perfect game, though the term itself was not used until 42 years later. Ward's (right) perfect game accounted for 1 of his 39 victories in 1880.

In a day when baseball players were from the rough-and-tumble side of the tracks, Ward, like Richmond, had a more genteel background, including a stint at Penn State (though he was kicked out after some hijinks involving stolen chickens). Even after becoming a professional "ballist," he continued his education, eventually earning a law degree while playing. He would use his legal training to help establish baseball's first players' union, the Brotherhood of Professional Base Ball Players in 1885 and the short-lived Players' League in 1890.

But back to 1880, when Ward was in his fourth pro season, and Richmond his first. Each pitched more than 590 innings; Ward had 39 wins, and Richmond ended with 32. Ward's eight shutouts were a league best.

Richmond (left). Ward (right) in action for the Providence Grays.

On June 17, Ward, pitching for the Providence Grays, took the hill at home against Buffalo. It was an odd 11:00 A.M. start, arranged to give the fans a chance to get the game in and still have time to watch a regatta planned for that afternoon. An investigation by historian Frederick Ivor-Campbell some years ago showed that the time change benefited Ward by putting the sun more directly into the batters' eyes.

In an odd quirk of the time, Providence batted first on its home field, the result of the then-traditional pregame coin flip. The Grays were facing a future Hall of Famer on the mound in the person of Pud Galvin (it would be the only perfect game in which a future Hall of Famer took the loss). They scratched out a run in the second, and added single runs in the fourth, seventh, eighth, and ninth.

Contemporary records do not note any spectacular defensive plays in Ward's support, but only five balls were hit to the outfield all day. His teammates' performances were perhaps the more remarkable of the day; earlier in the season, Providence had made 11 errors in one game.

And all of a sudden, that was that, a 5–0 win by Providence in which no Buffalo runners reached base. There was no postgame hoopla, little celebration in the press beyond a few superlatives. Five days after Richmond did it first, Ward did it second, and almost no one noticed.

Amazingly, on July 23, after giving up a leadoff single to Buffalo, Ward then allowed no base runners the rest of the way, thus nearly becoming the only pitcher with two perfect games . . . and both in one season.

A Slightly Different Game

The names of the teams were not the only unfamiliar things about these first two perfect games. The very rules under which the games were played varied a bit from what today's fans are used to seeing.

Instead of a mound 60 feet, six inches from home plate, pitchers threw from flat ground, their feet in a box whose front edge was 45 feet from home plate. Those pitchers did not throw overhand as pitchers do today, but by rule, could not raise their arms above their shoulders to throw the ball.

They could not throw it anywhere they wanted either. Batters indicated either a high (above the waist) or low (below the waist) zone; if a pitch was over the plate, but missed the selected zone, it was a ball. It helped pitchers that a walk was achieved after eight balls in 1880 (it lowered incrementally to four by 1889). Three strikes was still an out, but foul balls of any sort were not counted. (A bonus for the defense was that foul balls could be caught on one bounce—a "foul bound"—to record an out.)

Of course, with all this, pitchers still had to go out there practically every day. Richmond told of pitching 13 games in one 13-day stretch. Teams had perhaps one "change pitcher," but injury was usually the only way he'd make an appearance.

It was a different game, for sure, but that should not detract from Richmond's groundbreaking success.

Ward's career after the perfect game is almost as remarkable. After winning 164 games and notching the fourth-best ERA of all time (2.10), arm injuries chased him from the mound. So he moved to shortstop and played most of 11 more seasons there, becoming one of the best all-around players of the day (including a league-leading 111 stolen bases in 1887). He even played some outfield to give his arm a rest . . . and played left-handed. Ward's double-duty success as a pitcher and field player are surpassed perhaps only by Babe Ruth.

One question remains about the double perfectos: did Ward know about Richmond's feat when he accomplished the same thing? All the evidence says that he did not. Ward's biographer, Bryan di Salvatore, says, "There was no indication I could find that Ward knew of Richmond's game. I would be extremely surprised if Ward had any awareness of it."

Now, of course, 125 years later, the two men are well-known to all of baseball as the first to accomplish baseball's rarest pitching feat, the perfect game.

JOHN M. WARD'S PERFECT GAME
JUNE 17, 1880

Providence	AB	R	H	RBI
Hines, cf	5	0	2	NA
Start, 1b	5	1	1	-
Dorgan, rf	5	0	2	-
Gross, c	5	0	0	-
Farrell, 2b	4	3	3	-
Ward, p	4	0	1	-
Peters, ss	4	0	1	-
York, lf	4	0	2	-
Bradley, 3b	4	1	1	-
Totals	40	5	13	-

Buffalo	AB	R	H	RBI
Crowley, rf/c	3	0	0	NA
Richardson, 3b	3	0	0	-
Rowe, c/rf	3	0	0	-
Walker, lf	3	0	0	-
Hornung, 2b	3	0	0	-
Mack, ss	3	0	0	-
Esterbrook, 1b	3	0	0	-
Poorman, cf	3	0	0	-
Galvin, p	3	0	0	-
Totals	27	0	0	-

	1	2	3	4	5	6	7	8	9	R	H	E
Prv	0	1	0	1	0	0	1	1	1	5	13	0
Buf	0	0	0	0	0	0	0	0	0	0	0	7

Providence	IP	H	R	ER	BB	K
Ward (W)	9.0	0	0	0	0	2

Buffalo	IP	H	R	ER	BB	K
Galvin (L)	9.0	13	5	3	0	2

CHAPTER 2

Ahead of His Time

CHAPTER 3

It seems only fitting that "modern" baseball's first perfect game came from a pitcher who remains today as a symbol of pitching greatness. By 1904, when Cy Young pitched his perfect game, baseball had two major leagues and the game was played under essentially the same rules as today's game (the DH being one obvious difference). By 1904, all foul balls were strikes (except the third one), which had not been true up until 1903.

But while 15 others have matched the feat in the 100 years since Cy Young threw his perfect game, no pitcher has come close to matching his career record of 511 wins, a mark that today seems as unapproachable as any in sports. Consider that through 2004, Roger Clemens remains in the game today as a 300-game winner pitching in the majors, and the Rocket will certainly never fly as high as Young in wins. Young's longevity (1890–1911, 22 seasons) and his success over that long haul combined to make him one of the first members of the Hall of Fame and the source for the name of the annual pitching award in each league.

Yet when Young threw his perfect game, in Boston for the hometown Americans against the Philadelphia Athletics, no one realized just what a historic occasion it was. In fact, it would be nearly 20 years before anyone figured out just what to call it. Perhaps the only thing that wasn't perfect about modern baseball's first perfect game was that it didn't have a name.

Young and the Americans entered that 1904 season as the defending champions of the very first World Series. He had won two games in that Series victory over Pittsburgh, following a league-leading 28 victories on the season. He was at the peak of his pitching prowess, and his victory total of 379 entering 1904 was already the most in history. Victory number 380 would prove to be among his most important and most memorable. But what is less known is that the nine innings of his perfect game were part of a nearly unmatched streak of another kind.

Young and the Americans (they became the Red Sox in 1907) welcomed the Athletics to a packed Huntington Avenue Grounds. The 10,267 fans who packed the wooden seats and bleachers made up the largest regular-season crowd in the club's three-year history. Part of the attraction was the mound matchup between Young and the A's mercurial fireballer Rube Waddell. Waddell, whose 349 strikeouts that season would set a record that would stand for 61 years, had beaten Young and the Bostons on April 25 and then again on May 2 (with Jesse Tannehill pitching for Boston).

That record crowd enjoyed a very quick and quiet first few innings. Boston scratched out six hits, while the Athletics all went down meekly. Well, mostly

meekly. Right fielder Buck Freeman had to "tear in from right like a deer," according to Young, to snag a short pop-up behind second base.

Chick Stahl led off the Boston sixth with a triple to deep right field. Buck Freeman followed with another, and Young had the only run he would need. In the seventh, Young got some help from Pat Dougherty in left, who chased down a long foul into the corner. Shortstop Freddie Parent clocked the third out of the inning by charging a slow roller. In the bottom of the seventh, after Boston added another run, Young helped his own cause. A's shortstop Danny Murphy couldn't handle Young's grounder and the third run scored.

Though at this point in baseball history it had been 24 years since a perfect game had been pitched, no-hitters were certainly a recognized feat. And though the Huntington Grounds did not boast a scoreboard, fans were beginning to realize that their hero was holding the enemy hitless. Their cheers in the eighth and ninth, contemporary accounts say, rose with each pitch and batter and out.

Ironically, Young faced Waddell himself in search of the 27th out.

"I never worked harder in my life than I did for those last outs," Young said after the game. "After Parent helped me out by getting Schreck's [Philly catcher Ossie Schreckengost] grounder, it was up to me to go for earnest, and Waddell was the man. I sized him and let go."

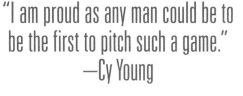

"I am proud as any man could be to be the first to pitch such a game."
—Cy Young

Waddell hit Young's third pitch and sent a lazy fly to center and Young to baseball history. It was over and modern baseball had its first-ever perfect game.

Said the *Boston Post*, in prose still evocative of the times: "As [the ball] dropped into Stahl's glove, a roar as if a hundred cannons had belched forth across the stands and bleachers; staid professional and business men fell over each other to congratulate Young and the Boston players."

Fans did indeed fill the field to surround their no-hit pitcher. Young wrote later of one fellow who pressed a $5 bill into his hand on the field.

"I wouldn't have missed that for a hundred dollars," Waddell said in sportsmanlike fashion.

It quickly became apparent to everyone present that what they had seen was more than a mere no-hitter. "Not a Quaker Reached First Base," read the *Boston Post* headline the next day. "I am proud as any man could be to be the first to pitch such a game," Young was quoted as saying. The press lauded the game and a few days later dug up accounts of Richmond and Ward to compare it to.

"The most wonderful game of ball in the annals of the American sport," wrote the *Boston Post*.

But no one called it "perfect."

About his other streak: Young entered the Athletics game on a 14-inning scoreless streak (the final seven innings of a start and seven innings from a rare

Young threw his perfect game for the Boston Americans in 1904.

relief stint). He followed perfection with a 15-inning shutout of Detroit. On May 17, he pitched 7⅔ scoreless before finally giving up a run to Cleveland. Including his nine perfect innings at Boston, Young's scoreless-innings streak was 45 innings. Several other pitchers since have put together longer streaks—the current record-holder is Orel Hershiser with 59 straight in 1988—but none included a perfect game. Plus, of Young's 45 innings, 24 of them in a row were hitless—in effect nearly three straight no-hitters. Not even Johnny Vander Meer matched that mark, though several relief pitchers have prevented hits for longer stints.

The name of this book is *Unhittable*, and as much as any pitcher in history—Big Trains, Leftys, Rockets, and others—Cy Young was just that for a splendid spring in 1904.

Young, shown here as a Cleveland Indian, still holds major league records for victories (511) and complete games (749).

CY YOUNG'S PERFECT GAME
MAY 5, 1904

Philadelphia	AB	R	H	RBI
Hartsell, lf	1	0	0	0
Hoffman, lf	2	0	0	0
Pickering, cf	3	0	0	0
Davis, 1b	3	0	0	0
L. Cross, 3b	3	0	0	0
Seybold, rf	3	0	0	0
Murphy, 2b	3	0	0	0
M. Cross, ss	3	0	0	0
Schreckengost, c	3	0	0	0
Waddell, p	3	0	0	0
Totals	**27**	**0**	**0**	**0**

Boston	AB	R	H	RBI
Collins, 3b	4	0	2	0
Stahl, cf	4	1	1	0
Freeman, rf	4	0	1	1
Parent, ss	4	0	2	0
LaChance, 1b	3	0	1	0
Ferris, 2b	3	1	1	0
Criger, c	3	1	1	1
Young, p	3	0	0	1
Totals	**32**	**3**	**10**	**3**

	1	2	3		4	5	6		7	8	9		R	H	E
Phil	0	0	0		0	0	0		0	0	0		0	0	1
Bos	0	0	0		0	0	1		2	0	x		3	10	0

Philadelphia	IP	H	R	ER	BB	K
Waddell (L)	8	10	3	3	0	6

Boston	IP	H	R	ER	BB	K
Young (W)	9	0	0	0	0	3

Time—1:25; Att.—10,267

Going for Two

No pitcher has thrown two perfect games, but Young came about as close as you can. In 1908, at the age of 41, Young tossed a no-hitter, his third. He faced the New York Highlanders and enjoyed great run support to win 8–0. What makes Young's feat that day special was what happened in the first inning. He walked the leadoff batter, Harry Niles, who was caught stealing. Young then retired the next 26 batters in a row. He was a walk away from perfection. Only John M. Ward, Addie Joss, and Sandy Koufax came as close to two perfect games by pitching no-hitters with but a single blemish.

At age 37 in 1904, Young was the oldest pitcher ever to throw a perfect game until 40-year-old Randy Johnson topped him in 2004 (see Chapter 37). Young's 1908 no-hitter still makes him the second oldest behind Nolan Ryan (age 44 in 1991) to toss a no-hitter.

Though he competed a century ago, most modern experts still list Young among the all-time pitching greats.

Rising to the Occasion

It's baseball's annual showcase event, a living melodrama in seven acts or less, witnessed by millions across the globe through the magic of television. Everything is magnified. Indelible impressions are formed. Reputations are made. Careers are tainted.

Reggie Jackson hits three home runs in one World Series game and "Mr. October" is born. Mickey Owen drops a third strike. Don Larsen, the Imperfect Man, pitches a perfect game. Johnny Pesky holds on to a baseball a split second and the winning run crosses the plate. Willie Mays catches Vic Wertz' drive with his back to home plate. Bill Buckner lets a ground ball trickle through his legs. Bill Wambsganss makes an unassisted triple play. Charlie Root gives up Babe Ruth's called shot. Dusty Rhodes drives in six runs with two pinch-hit singles and a pinch-hit home run.

Historically, pitchers have dominated the World Series, from the mediocre ones (Larsen, Bill Bevens, Johnny Beazley, Johnny Kucks, Larry Sherry, and Moe Drabowsky) who succeeded in their one stab at

> Gibson's seven-game World Series winning streak was over, but his eight strikeouts in Game 7 gave him a Series record of 35 Ks.

the brass ring, to the great ones (Christy Mathewson, Whitey Ford, Sandy Koufax, Bob Gibson, Catfish Hunter, and Randy Johnson) who validated their status with their World Series performances.

Mathewson, the New York Giants college-educated pitching ace who four times won 30 games or more in a season and is tied for third on the all-time list with 373 wins, was the first World Series hero in the second Series ever played, in 1905. He set a standard that has not been equaled in a century of World Series by pitching three shutouts in six days against the Philadelphia Athletics, allowing just 14 hits, walking one, and striking out 18 in 27 innings.

Twelve other pitchers have won three games in one World Series, but none came close to shutting down a Series opponent like the great Matty, and only Jack Coombs of the Philadelphia Athletics against the Chicago Cubs in 1910, like Mathewson, won three games in a five-game Series.

Mathewson threw three straight World Series shutouts to lead New York to the 1905 title.

Gibson still holds the record after fanning 17 Tigers in the 1968 Series.

The last pitcher to win three games in a Series was Randy Johnson of the Arizona Diamondbacks against the New York Yankees in 2001, with one win coming in relief. The last pitcher to win three starts was Mickey Lolich of the Detroit Tigers against the St. Louis Cardinals in 1968. Interestingly, when he squared off against Bob Gibson in the seventh game, each had thrown two complete game victories.

Coming off a sensational regular season in which he won 22 games, pitched 13 shutouts, and posted an earned run average of 1.12, Gibson set a still standing World Series record by striking out 17, beating the Tigers and 31-game-winner Denny McLain 4–0 in Game 1.

Lolich evened the Series with an 8–1, complete game victory in Game 2. The Cardinals won the third game and Gibson put his team up, three games to one, with a complete game 10–1 victory in Game 4. He struck out 10 and ran his World Series winning streak to seven consecutive games.

Lolich got his second win in Game 5, and in the sixth game, McLain got his only World Series victory to even the Series at three games apiece, setting up the Gibson-Lolich confrontation in Game 7 in St. Louis.

With Gibson pitching on three days' rest and Lolich on two days' rest, the two studs went into the seventh inning scoreless. Gibson, who had won three games in the World Series against the Boston Red Sox the previous year and seventh games in the 1964 and 1967 World Series, was on the mound in the top of the seventh. The game turned when the normally impeccable Cardinals center fielder Curt Flood misplayed a drive by Jim Northrup into a two-run triple.

Lolich held the Cardinals scoreless until the ninth, when Mike Shannon hit a two-out home run to spoil the shutout. The Tigers won 4–1, and Lolich joined Mathewson, Smokey Joe Wood, Stan Coveleskie, Harry "the Cat" Brecheen, Lew Burdette, and Gibson among pitchers who have won three games in a World Series.

Gibson's seven-game World Series winning streak was over, but his eight strikeouts in Game 7 gave him a Series record of 35 Ks.

Don Larsen's perfect game against the Brooklyn Dodgers in 1956 stands as the greatest pitching performance in World Series history—probably the greatest World Series performance of any kind (see Chapter 17). Before Larsen, three pitchers had come close to World Series immortality, and one of them was a loser.

In Game 2 of the 1906 World Series, the Chicago White Sox scored their only run against the Chicago Cubs' Ed Reulbach in the fifth inning without a hit, and were hitless until Jiggs Donahue singled in the seventh. Reulbach won the game, 7–1, on a one-hitter.

Morris' epic Game 7 victory in 1991 goes down as one of the all-time great World Series pitching performances.

Koufax, celebrating with catcher John Roseboro, beat the Yankees 2–1 in Game 4 to complete a Dodgers sweep in the 1963 World Series.

Bevens (left) and Joe DiMaggio exit Brooklyn's Ebbets Field in shock after Bevens lost his no-hitter—and the game—to the Dodgers in the ninth inning of Game 4 in 1947.

In Game 3 in 1945, another Cub, Claude Passeau, gave up a hit to Rudy York of the Tigers in the second inning and then held Detroit hitless the remainder of the game, a 3–0 Cubs victory.

Two years later, Bill Bevens of the Yankees, who had won only seven games during the regular season and had a career record of 40–36, carried a no-hitter against the Dodgers into the ninth inning of Game 4 at Brooklyn's Ebbets Field. The Yankees led 2–1 as Bevens' wildness—he walked 10—enabled the Dodgers to score without a hit in the fifth.

A one-out walk to Carl Furillo, a stolen base, and a two-out intentional walk to Pete Reiser put Dodgers on first and second. Cookie Lavagetto, batting for Eddie Stanky, doubled high off the right field screen to score two runs and make Bevens the all-time World Series heartbreak loser. Bevens never started another game in the major leagues.

Grover Cleveland Alexander, the man they called "Old Pete," was on the downside of his fabulous career when he was traded to the St. Louis Cardinals on June 22, 1926. Alexander would win 373 games and pitch 90 shutouts in the major leagues, but it had been three years since he had won 22 for the Cubs, and nine years since he completed a string of three straight years with 30 wins or more for the Phillies. He was 39 years old and an epileptic.

The previous season, he was 15–11 for the Cubs, and when the Cardinals got him, his record was 3–3. But Old Pete would use his experience and his guile to win nine games the remainder of the season and help St. Louis win its first baseball championship in 38 years. Now Alexander was taking the mound in brand-new Yankee Stadium to face the game's newest powerhouse, the fearsome Yankees of Babe Ruth, Lou Gehrig, Bob Meusel, and Tony Lazzeri in Game 2 of the 1926 World Series.

Old Pete pitched courageously, striking out 10 and allowing just two runs and four hits (among them, Ruth, Gehrig, Meusel, and Lazzeri had just two singles in 14 at-bats) in a 6–2 Cardinals victory.

Alexander returned to the Yankee Stadium mound to start Game 6 with the Yankees leading the Series, three games to two. Again he pitched a complete game. Again he kept the Yankees' bats in check (Ruth and Lazzeri were hitless in seven at-bats) and beat the Yanks 10–2, allowing eight hits and striking out six.

When the game was over, Old Pete found his favorite New York watering hole and partied into the night, thinking his year's work was done. Jesse Haines would pitch the seventh game for the Cards against Waite Hoyt, and Alexander would rest his tired arm in the bullpen.

In the seventh inning, with the Cardinals clinging to a 3–2 lead, Haines developed a blister on the index finger of his pitching hand, and the Yankees loaded the bases with two outs and the rookie Lazzeri coming to bat.

Cardinals manager Rogers Hornsby knew it was time for a pitching change, and who better to call upon in such a critical situation than his time-tested veteran, Old Pete?

The count went to 1–1 and Lazzeri hit the next pitch on a blistering line to left field, just foul by inches. Alexander blew the next pitch past the rookie, who swung and missed for strike three, leaving three runners stranded. Alexander retired the Yankees in order in the eighth and faced the top of the Yankees batting order in the ninth, protecting the Cardinals' one-run lead.

Earle Combs grounded to third. Mark Koenig grounded to third. That brought up Ruth. Alexander ran the count full and then walked the mighty Babe.

What happened next was one of the most bizarre and mysterious plays in World Series history. With Meusel, a feared slugger who had led the American League with 33 home runs the year before, at bat, Ruth inexplicably took off for second base. Catcher Bob O'Farrell fired a strike to second baseman Hornsby, Ruth was out attempting to steal second, and Alexander had triumphed in perhaps the finest moment of a brilliant career.

No discussion of World Series pitching prowess would be complete without mention of Sandy Koufax in the 1963 and 1965 Series, Jack Morris in the 1991 Series, and the dynamic duo of Randy Johnson and Curt Schilling in the 2001 Series.

In 1963, Koufax had his breakout season. He won 25 games, had an ERA of 1.88, 20 complete games, 11 shutouts, and 306 strikeouts in 311 innings. He would be the focal point of the World Series between Koufax's Dodgers and the Yankees of Mickey Mantle, Roger Maris, and Whitey Ford.

Ford, whose 10 victories were the most in World Series history, and who had broken a World Series record held by Babe Ruth by pitching 33²/₃ consecutive scoreless innings from 1960 to 1962, hooked up with Koufax in Game 1 at Yankee Stadium. Koufax established his dominance immediately by striking out the first five Yankees. He took a shutout into the eighth inning, when Tom Tresh blasted a two-run homer into the left-field seats. But Koufax won the game 5–2, ending it by fanning pinch-hitter Harry Bright for his 15th strikeout, breaking the record of 14 set by another Dodgers pitcher, Carl Erskine, also against the Yankees, 10 years before.

When the Dodgers won Game 2, they returned to Los Angeles with 19-game winner Don Drysdale rested and ready for Game 3 and Koufax penciled in for Game 4.

In the third game, the Dodgers scored a run in the first and Drysdale let it stand up the rest of the way for a 1–0 victory. Drysdale limited the Yankees to three hits and struck out nine, and the Yankees knew they had to beat Koufax the next day just to stay alive.

"Isn't there a Jewish holiday coming up?" wondered third baseman Clete Boyer.

There wasn't. Again it was Koufax against Ford. Again Koufax got the upper hand. Frank Howard homered off Ford in the fifth. Mantle homered off Koufax in the seventh to tie. Willie Davis' sacrifice fly in the bottom of the seventh put the Dodgers back on top, 2–1. And Koufax closed the deal. He held the Yankees to two hits and struck out eight, giving him 23 strikeouts, a record for a four-game Series.

The Dodgers had beaten the Yankees with ridiculous ease, a four-game sweep dominated by pitching. In the four games, Dodgers pitchers struck out 37 Yankees, allowed four runs, 22 hits, and held them to a team batting average of .171.

Two years later, the Dodgers faced the Minnesota Twins in the World Series. This time, there was a Jewish holiday, Yom Kippur, and Koufax sat out the opening game as the Twins beat the Dodgers 8–2. Koufax started Game 2 against Jim Kaat, but Koufax was not on his game. He

CHAPTER 4

Johnson and Schilling pulled out all the stops in 2001 to deliver the KO punch to the favored Yankees.

lasted six innings and although he struck out nine, was reached for two runs and six hits, and the Dodgers lost 5–1.

Down two games to none, their backs to the wall, the Dodgers returned to Los Angeles and got a lift in the form of a shutout by left-hander Claude Osteen for a 4–0 victory in Game 3. Drysdale won Game 4, 7–2, to tie the Series at two games apiece, and Koufax was his masterful self in Game 5. The Dodgers knocked Kaat out in the third, while Koufax limited the Twins to four singles and struck out 10 in a 7–0 victory.

When the Twins won Game 6, Dodgers manager Walter Alston decided to bypass Drysdale and bring Koufax back in Game 7 on two days' rest. Again, he was brilliant. He struck out 10, allowed three hits, and beat the Twins, 2–0, giving him a string of 18 consecutive scoreless innings.

Jack Morris had won 198 games, plus two in the 1984 World Series, in a 14-year career with the Detroit Tigers. Now he was going home, signed by the hometown Minnesota Twins after the 1990 season.

Morris, a battle-tested 36 years old, won 18 games for the Twins in 1991, and then he won two games over the Blue Jays in the American League Championship Series to help Minnesota get to the World Series. There they met up with the Atlanta Braves, a match-up of two teams that had finished in last place the previous year.

Morris won Game 1, 5–2. In Game 4 he left after six innings, having allowed just one run, and was not involved in the decision. When the Series was tied after six games, Morris came back to start Game 7 with three days' rest against 24-year-old John Smoltz, a native of Detroit who grew up idolizing Morris, the Tigers' ace.

Morris and Smoltz battled through seven scoreless innings in one of the classic pitching duels in World Series history. When Lonnie Smith led off the Atlanta eighth with a single and Terry Pendleton followed with a drive off the wall in left center, it appeared that the Braves would break the scoreless deadlock. But Smith stumbled going around second and was held up at third. Morris had to face the heart of the Braves batting order with no outs and runners on second and third.

He induced Ron Gant to ground to first baseman Kent Hrbek, who held the runners and stepped on the bag for the first out. Twins ma-nager Tom Kelly ordered David Justice intentionally walked to load the bases. Morris then got Sid Bream to hit to first baseman Hrbek, who fired home to force Smith, and then took the return throw from catcher Brian Harper to complete the inning-ending double play and keep the game scoreless.

The Twins also loaded the bases in the bottom of the eighth, and they too failed to score when Hrbek hit into an inning-ending double play. Smoltz had been removed from the game in the bottom of the eighth, but Morris pressed on. He retired the Braves in order in the ninth and tenth, and the Twins batted in the bottom of the tenth.

A leadoff double by Dan Gladden, a sacrifice bunt, and two intentional walks loaded the bases for Minnesota with one out. Pinch-hitter Gene Larkin drove a ball over the drawn-in outfield to give the Twins the victory in only the second (the Yankees and Giants in 1962) 1–0 World Series seventh game ever played. It also raised Morris' postseason record to 7–1.

Johnson and Schilling were the 1-2 punch that stymied the Yankees to win the 2001 World Series, after combining for five of the Arizona Diamondbacks' seven playoff victories that got them to the big show.

Schilling beat the Yankees' in Game 1, 9–1, and Johnson pitched a shutout to win Game 2. When the Yankees won the next three games in New York to take a 3–2 lead, the Diamondbacks returned home for the final two games, relying on their 1-2 pitching punch.

Johnson, "the Big Unit," started Game 6 and the D-backs exploded for a 15–2 romp. With the huge lead, Johnson left after seven innings and would be ready in relief for Game 7, if he was needed.

He was needed. With the Yankees leading 2–1 in the eighth, Johnson relieved on the day after he had started, got the final out of the inning, then retired the side in order in the ninth. When the Diamondbacks rallied for two in the bottom of the ninth off the Yankees' peerless reliever, Mariano Rivera, Arizona had won its first World Series and Randy Johnson had become the first pitcher since Mickey Lolich in 1968 to win three games in one World Series.

Between them, Schilling and Johnson pitched in five of the seven games. In a combined $38^2/_3$ innings, they allowed six runs, 21 hits, and struck out 45.

All in a Day's Work

In the 32-year history of the National League, there had never been a pennant race like it—three teams, the New York Giants, Pittsburgh Pirates, and powerhouse, two-time defending champion Chicago Cubs of "Tinker-to-Evers-to-Chance" fame—pounding neck and neck down the stretch.

All three had taken a turn leading the league in the previous week, and on the morning of September 26, 1908, the top of the National League standings looked like this:

	W–L	GB
Chicago	91–54	–
Pittsburgh	91–55	⅟₂
New York	88–52	⅟₂

And when he also won the second game, 3—0, in a snappy one hour and 12 minutes, allowing three hits and four walks and striking out four, he had done what no pitcher in baseball history had ever done—not even Iron Man McGinnity.

The Cubs, who had won 223 games and finished 20 and 17 games ahead of the field in the previous two seasons, were in trouble. Their pitching staff was in shambles, weary from the stretch run and wracked with injury, as they prepared to face the Brooklyn Dodgers in a doubleheader.

Manager Frank Chance, strapped for starting pitchers, was in a quandary. Mordecai "Three-Finger" Brown, his ace, and Orval Overall had each started twice in the last four days. Jack Pfiester's strong effort just three days earlier had been wasted, a 1–1 tie with the Giants. Chance had "Big" Ed Reulbach ready to start the first game in Brooklyn, but what about the second game?

"I'll pitch both games," volunteered Reulbach, who had earned a reputation as a workhorse in 1905, his rookie year, when he started 29 games, completed 28, pitched in relief five times, worked 292 innings, and won 18 games.

In those days, starting both ends of a doubleheader was rare for a pitcher, but not unprecedented. Five years earlier, Joe McGinnity of the New York Giants not only started both games of a doubleheader three times, but he won all six games and pitched six complete games, earning him the nickname "Iron Man."

Reulbach spent much of his career in the shadows of two other Chicago pitching greats, but he answered the call like no other in the heat of the 1908 pennant race.

ED REULBACH'S DOUBLEHEADER GAME 1 SHUTOUT
SEPTEMBER 26, 1908

Chicago	AB	R	H	RBI
Hayden, rf	4	0	0	1
Evers, 2b	4	1	2	1
Schulte, lf	4	0	0	0
Chance, 1b	4	0	0	0
Steinfeldt, 3b	4	1	3	1
Hofman, cf	4	0	1	1
Tinker, ss	4	1	1	0
Kling, c	4	2	3	1
Reulbach, p	2	0	0	0
Totals	**34**	**5**	**10**	**5**

Brooklyn	AB	R	H	RBI
Catterson, lf	4	0	0	0
Lumley, rf	4	0	0	0
Hummel, 2b	4	0	1	0
Jordan, 1b	3	0	0	0
Burch, cf	4	0	0	0
McMillan, ss	3	0	1	0
Sheehan, 3b	3	0	1	0
Dunn, c	3	0	2	0
Wilhelm, p	3	0	0	0
Totals	**31**	**0**	**5**	**0**

	1	2	3	4	5	6	7	8	9	R	H	E
Chi	0	0	0	0	1	0	1	2	1	5	10	0
Br	0	0	0	0	0	0	0	0	0	0	5	4

Chicago	IP	H	R	ER	BB	K
Reulbach (W)	9	5	0	0	1	7

Brooklyn	IP	H	R	ER	BB	K
Wilhelm (L)	9	10	5	4	1	5

Time—1:40

ED REULBACH'S DOUBLEHEADER GAME 2 SHUTOUT
SEPTEMBER 26, 1908

Chicago	AB	R	H	RBI
Hayden, rf	4	1	1	0
Evers, 2b	4	0	1	0
Schulte, lf	2	0	1	0
Chance, 1b	4	0	0	0
Steinfeldt, 3b	4	0	0	0
Hofman, cf	3	0	0	0
Tinker, ss	3	0	0	0
Kling, c	3	1	2	0
Reulbach, p	1	1	0	1
Totals	**28**	**3**	**5**	**1**

Brooklyn	AB	R	H	RBI
Catterson, lf	4	0	1	0
Lumley, rf	4	0	2	0
Hummel, 2b	4	0	0	0
Jordan, 1b	3	0	0	0
Burch, cf	3	0	0	0
McMillan, ss	3	0	0	0
Sheehan, 3b	3	0	0	0
Dunn, c	3	0	0	0
Pastorius, p	2	0	0	0
Pattee, ph	1	0	0	0
Totals	**30**	**0**	**3**	**0**

	1	2	3	4	5	6	7	8	9	R	H	E
Chi	0	0	1	0	0	0	0	2	0	3	5	1
Br	0	0	0	0	0	0	0	0	0	0	3	3

Chicago	IP	H	R	ER	BB	K
Reulbach (W)	9	3	0	0	1	4

Brooklyn	IP	H	R	ER	BB	K
Pastorius (L)	9	5	3	1	3	2

Time—1:12; Att.15,000

For Reulbach, however, it was venturing into uncharted waters as he beat the Dodgers 5–0 in Game 1 on September 26, 1908. He held the opposition to five hits, walked one, and struck out six.

And when he also won the second game, 3–0, in a snappy one hour and 12 minutes, allowing three hits and four walks and striking out four, he had done what no pitcher in baseball history had ever done—not even Iron Man McGinnity. Reulbach had pitched shutouts in both games of a doubleheader.

When the Cubs and Giants had identical records at the end of the season, they were forced to meet in a replay of their game played on September 23, the famed "Merkle Boner" game, which had ended in a tie. In the playoff, the Cubs beat 37-game-winner Christy Mathewson, 4–2, and the standings at the top of the National League on October 9, 1908, looked like this:

	W–L	GB
Chicago	99–55	–
New York	98–56	1
Pittsburgh	98–56	1

Despite winning 24 games in 1908, pitching the first World Series one-hitter in 1906, and finishing with a lifetime record of 181–105, Reulbach never was accorded the recognition his career deserved. He spent his career overshadowed by his teammate, Three-Finger Brown, and crosstown rival, Big Ed Walsh.

But his feat of pitching two shutouts in one day has never been equaled . . . and, doubtless, never will be.

CHAPTER 5

CHAPTER 6

When Perfect Almost Wasn't Enough

It's one thing to throw a perfect game, with all of its attendant pressures and with the eyes of the baseball world upon you (more so today than ever, courtesy of ESPN and others). But it's another thing entirely to throw a perfect game when elimination from a pennant race is a possibility. Addie Joss' perfect game in 1908 is an example of just that: he came through with perfection when he had to, and when anything less might not have been enough.

Joss was a teenage pitching phenom in Ohio. His 1902 pro debut was nearly as spectacular as his 1908 perfecto. Other than a disputed hit (Joss' fielder claimed he had caught the ball; the umps disagreed), no St. Louis Browns reached base against Joss and his Cleveland team. Along with being a talented and versatile pitcher, Joss was intelligent enough to have been hired by the *Cleveland Press* as a sportswriter; he even covered several World Series for the paper.

Before he was 25, Joss was among the best pitchers in baseball, leading the AL with a 1.59 ERA in 1904 and with 27 wins in 1907. In 1908, however, he topped even his best performances to that time. His 1.16 ERA was one of the lowest of the century, and he allowed only 30 walks in 325 innings, the third-best ratio of all time (behind Walter Johnson in 1913 and Pedro Martinez in 2000).

The Cleveland team had taken the name "Naps" that year for its leader, the great hitter Napoleon Lajoie. They faced off against the White Sox on October 2, locked in one of baseball's tightest pennant races. Cleveland led Chicago by only a half game with four games to play. A loss would put the Naps in second place; a win would put them in great position to capture the flag.

Facing Joss was a pitcher of nearly equal skill. Ed Walsh had won 39 games that season with a 1.42 ERA. It is interesting to note that on the career ERA list, Walsh comes in first at 1.82, with Joss in second at 1.89. In this one game, the top two ERA men of all time faced off with a pennant on the line.

The first defensive gem came in the third (so many of the perfect games, though beautifully pitched, depended on teamwork and defense for final perfection). Walsh dribbled a ball to the right of the mound. Joss dived, missed, and then watched happily as Lajoie stormed in to make the throw to nab the runner.

In the bottom of the third, Cleveland centerfielder Joe Birmingham scored the game's only run. After singling, he danced off first, drawing a throw by Walsh. Birmingham was racing for second by that time, however. First baseman Frank Isbell's throw plunked the Naps runner and bounded into center, and Cleveland had a runner on third with no outs. With two outs, Walsh gave Joss the edge he would need, uncorking a wild pitch that scored Birmingham.

Joss was using his unusual windup (he turned, Luis Tiant–like, a half-turn toward second before spinning and releasing each pitch) and multiple arm angles to great effect.

After two times through the lineup, Joss was among several who recognized what was happening. "About the seventh inning, I began to realize that not one of the Sox had reached first base," he said after the game. "No one on the bench dared to breathe a word to that effect." According to the Cleveland papers, the players weren't the only quiet ones. In contrast to the raucous Boston crowds for Cy Young in 1904, Cleveland's fans were eerily quiet when Joss pitched.

In the ninth, one reporter said the only sound was the clicking of the telegraph operator sending out news of the game.

Nursing a 1–0 lead and well aware that the Naps needed a victory more than he needed a perfect game, Joss got a ground-out and a strikeout. The final batter, pinch-hitter John Anderson, smacked a liner that landed just foul. With two strikes, Anderson hit a bullet toward Naps third baseman Bill Bradley. It was Bradley's only chance of the game and he nearly blew it. He chested the one-hopper and scrabbled in the dirt for the ball. His throw was low, and first baseman George Stovall was unable to field it cleanly, but did manage to keep the ball in front of him. With Anderson still heading toward first from home, Stovall had the split second he needed to pick up the ball before umpire Francis "Silk" O'Loughlin rang up the runner to conclude Joss' perfect game.

Joss and his teammates were taking no chances and, with the crowd now screaming, released from their self-imposed silence, and in pursuit, sprinted toward the centerfield clubhouse.

There Lajoie, a future Hall of Famer, was quoted as calling it the "best game I ever saw and the best game I ever took part in."

Three years later, while trying to rebound from an arm injury that had caused him to miss most of 1909 and 1910, Joss showed up for spring training. He fainted on April 3. Ill, he returned home to Toledo, where doctors discovered the terrible news. On April 14, two days after his 31st birthday, Addie Joss died of bacterial meningitis.

> Before he was 25, Joss was among the best pitchers in baseball, leading the AL with a 1.59 ERA in 1904 and with 27 wins in 1907.

Joss had to be virtually perfect to beat White Sox great "Big" Ed Walsh late in the 1908 season.

ADDIE JOSS' PERFECT GAME
OCTOBER 2, 1908

Chicago	AB	R	H	RBI
Hahn, rf	3	0	0	0
Jones, cf	3	0	0	0
Isbell, 1b	3	0	0	0
Dougherty, lf	3	0	0	0
Davis, 2b	3	0	0	0
Parent, ss	3	0	0	0
Schreckengost, c	2	0	0	0
Shaw, c	0	0	0	0
White, ph	1	0	0	0
Tannehill, 3b	2	0	0	0
Donahue, ph	1	0	0	0
Walsh, p	2	0	0	0
Anderson, ph	1	0	0	0
Totals	**27**	**0**	**0**	**0**

Cleveland	AB	R	H	RBI
Good, rf	4	0	0	0
Bradley, 3b	4	0	0	0
Hinchman, lf	3	0	0	0
Lajoie, 2b	3	0	1	0
Stovall, 1b	3	0	0	0
Clarke, c	3	0	0	0
Birmingham, cf	3	1	2	0
Perring, ss	2	0	1	0
Joss, p	3	0	0	1
Totals	**28**	**1**	**4**	**0**

	1	2	3	4	5	6	7	8	9	R	H	E
Chi	0	0	0	0	0	0	0	0	0	0	0	1
Cle	0	0	1	0	0	0	0	0	x	1	4	0

Chicago	IP	H	R	ER	BB	K
Walsh (L)	8	4	1	0	1	15

Cleveland	IP	H	R	ER	BB	K
Joss (W)	9	0	0	0	0	3

Time—1:32; Att.—10,598

Cleveland's Addie Joss.

Two for the Show

The year was 1917. World War I, the "war to end all wars," had been raging for three long years in Europe. On the home front, Woodrow Wilson was beginning his second term as the 28th president of the United States, and the game of baseball was going through a renaissance of sorts, as 1917 would come to be known as "The Year of the Pitcher."

Pitchers dominated the season. In the National League, Grover Cleveland Alexander of Philadelphia won 30 games and pitched to an earned run average of 1.86. In two years, Ed Cicotte of the Chicago White Sox would be implicated in the worst scandal in baseball history, but this year he would lead the American League with 28 wins and an ERA of 1.53. In Boston, a 22-year-old left-hander for the Red Sox named George Herman "Babe" Ruth was making a name for himself by winning 24 games (giving him 47 wins in two seasons) and completing 35 games.

There would be six no-hitters pitched in major league baseball in 1917, the most in one season in the game's modern era.

There would be six no-hitters pitched in major league baseball in 1917, the most in one season in the game's modern era.

Already by May 2, as Fred Toney of the Cincinnati Reds and James "Hippo" Vaughn of the Cubs prepared to face each other in Chicago's Weeghman Park (later known as Wrigley Field), two no-hitters had been thrown—on April 14 by Cicotte against St. Louis, and on April 24 by George Mogridge of the Yankees against Boston.

Toney and Vaughn would battle all season for the runner-up position to Alexander for the most wins in the National League, and their duel on May 2 was a microcosm of their season-long battle.

The Reds entered the game having failed to score a run in their previous 24 innings. In an effort to break the slump, Christy Mathewson, the immortal pitcher and now Cincinnati manager, started an all-right-handed hitting lineup against the southpaw, Vaughn. Mathewson benched his best hitter, Edd Roush, who would lead the National League with a .341 average. The strategy backfired as the Reds failed to get a hit through nine innings, and the only ball they hit to the outfield was caught by center fielder Cy Williams a few feet behind second base.

Vaughn gave up the only hit in the tenth and watched as two errors led to the winning run.

Toney finished the 1917 season with 24 victories, but none was more memorable than the historic no-hitter he threw on May 2.

JAMES VAUGHN/FRED TONEY DOUBLE NO-HITTER
MAY 2, 1917

Cincinnati	AB	R	H	RBI
Groh, 2b	1	0	0	0
Getz, 3b	1	0	0	0
Kopf, ss	4	1	1	0
Neale, cf	4	0	0	0
Chase, 1b	4	0	0	0
Thorpe, rf	4	0	1	1
Shean, 2b	3	0	0	0
Cueto, lf	3	0	0	0
Huhn, c	3	0	0	0
Toney, p	3	0	0	0
Totals	**30**	**1**	**2**	**1**

Chicago	AB	R	H	RBI
Zeider, ss	4	0	0	0
Walter, rf	4	0	0	0
Doyle, 2b	4	0	0	0
Merkle, 1b	4	0	0	0
Williams, cf	2	0	0	0
Mann, lf	3	0	0	0
Wilson, c	3	0	0	0
Deal, 3b	3	0	0	0
Vaughn, p	3	0	0	0
Totals	**30**	**0**	**0**	**0**

	1	2	3	4	5	6	7	8	9	10	R	H	E
Cin	0	0	0	0	0	0	0	0	0	1	1	2	0
Chi	0	0	0	0	0	0	0	0	0	0	0	0	2

Cincinnati	IP	H	R	ER	BB	K
Toney (W)	10	0	0	0	2	3

Chicago	IP	H	R	ER	BB	K
Vaughn (L)	10	2	1	0	2	10

Time—1:50

The oldest adage in baseball is "you can't win if you don't score," and through nine innings not only had the Reds failed to score, but they were also hitless against the Cincinnati right-hander, Toney.

Only once in baseball history had two no-hitters been pitched on the same day, and that came during the game's dark ages, April 22, 1898, when Ted Breitenstein of Cincinnati pitched his second no-hitter against Pittsburgh and James Hughes held Boston hitless for Baltimore.

Now two pitchers, in the same game, had each completed nine hitless innings.

Something had to give as Vaughn went out for the top of the tenth. With one out, Larry Kopf singled for the Reds against Vaughn, the game's first hit. It would be the game's only hit.

After Greasy Neale flied to center fielder Cy Williams for the second out, Williams muffed Hal Chase's fly ball for an error, putting runners on second and third. The next batter was the legendary Carlisle Indian and Olympic champion, Jim Thorpe, who topped a ball along the third-base line. Vaughn sprang from the mound, picked up the ball, and, realizing he had no chance to get the speedy Thorpe at first, fired home. The throw caught catcher Art Wilson by surprise, hitting him in the chest protector, and Kopf scored the game's only run.

Toney completed his no-hitter in the bottom of the tenth and Vaughn was the hard-luck loser of baseball's only double no-hit game and the greatest two-man pitching performance in baseball history.

"Wilson cried like a baby after the game," Vaughn said years later. "He grabbed my hand and said, 'I just went out on you, Jim; I just went tight.'"

Toney, a bear of a man at 6'6", and a workhorse who later that season would pitch and win both games of a doubleheader against Pittsburgh, would finish the season with 24 wins, one more than Vaughn.

But Vaughn would lead the National League in wins with 22 in 1918 and pitch three complete games in the 1918 World Series against the Red Sox, losing Game 1, 1–0, losing Game 3, 2–1, and winning Game 5, 3–0.

Toney made only one World Series appearance. He started Game 3 of the 1921 Series for the Giants against the Yankees and was knocked out in the third inning.

CHAPTER 7

What a Relief

You're the Boston Red Sox management in 1914. You've just obtained a trio of players from the Baltimore minor league franchise: a catcher named Ben Egan; a pitcher, Ernie Shore; and a pudgy kid named Ruth—Babe Ruth. Being the Red Sox, your first move is to bring one of them up to the majors. That's right: Ernie Shore.

Management straightened that out by 1915, and Shore and Ruth formed part of a pitching staff good enough to lead the Bosox to the World Series championship. But although they were teammates and shared a Baltimore past, the similarities ended there. Ruth was a slob; Shore wasn't (after rooming with Ruth, he requested a change). Ruth wasn't exactly a Rhodes Scholar; Shore was a schoolteacher. Ruth was a lefty, Shore a righty.

But for all their dissimilarities, they will be forever linked, thanks to Ruth's temper.

The Washington Senators were the visitors that summer day in 1917. Ruth came into the game on a roll, having shut out the Senators three days earlier while allowing no walks.

From then on Shore was Cy Young, Don Larsen, Jim Bunning, and David Cone, knocking off Senators as easily as a savings-and-loan scandal. The Red Sox gave Shore four runs and Shore gave Washington nothing. It was over quickly, less than two hours, and while Ruth was polishing off a postgame snack, Shore polished off what was considered the third recorded perfect game of the 20th century until 1991.

However, just as Shore's feat itself was overshadowed by the dominant personality of Ruth, who was not even around at the finish, so too is the feat overshadowed in history. An MLB rules committee in 1991 rewrote the rules defining a no-hitter, and by inclusion, perfect games. Shore's feat, while dominating, no longer officially qualified as a solo no-hitter and thus could not be a perfect game. (No-nos are officially a game in which the starter completes the game without allowing a hit. Shore's is now listed as a combined no-hitter, Ruth's walk having nixed the perfecto.)

While Shore's unhittable feat became a footnote to history, he is more remembered in Winston-Salem, North Carolina. His baseball career, followed by a long stint as a local sheriff, inspired townsfolk to name the minor-league park there for the pitcher who provided perhaps the best relief stint of all time.

> It was over quickly, less than two hours, and while Ruth was polishing off a postgame snack, Shore polished off what was considered the third recorded perfect game of the 20th century until 1991.

Ray Morgan, the Senators' second baseman and leadoff hitter, stepped to the plate and took ball one. He took ball two. And ball three. Ruth was getting steamed at home-plate umpire Brick Owens and, according to reports at the time, was pacing the mound and jawing at the ump.

Ball four. Morgan took first, and Ruth took off toward home. Owens tossed the future slugger quickly, and Ruth, in an act that would get him vilified today but only fined back then, slugged Owens in the side of the head.

After order was restored and the Babe sent to the showers, Babe's old roomie Shore was called in to pick up the pieces. He threw one pitch, Morgan broke for second, and Morgan was thrown out, though with less violence than Ruth.

Shore wasn't even expecting to take the hill on June 23, 1917, and the Senators surely wished he hadn't.

It was Ruth's undoing that led to the greatest relief performance of all time.

ERNIE SHORE'S PERFECT GAME IN RELIEF
JUNE 23, 1917

Washington	AB	R	H	RBI
Morgan, 2b	2	0	0	0
Foster, 3b	3	0	0	0
Leonard, 3b	0	0	0	0
Milan, cf	3	0	0	0
Rice, rf	3	0	0	0
Gharrity, 1b	0	0	0	0
Judge, 1b	3	0	0	0
Jamieson, lf	3	0	0	0
Shanks, ss	3	0	0	0
Henry, c	3	0	0	0
Ayers, p	2	0	0	0
Menosky, p	1	0	0	0
Totals	**26**	**0**	**0**	**0**

Boston	AB	R	H	RBI
Hooper, rf	4	0	1	2
Barry, 2b	4	0	0	0
Hoblitzell, 1b	4	0	0	0
Gardner, 3b	4	1	1	0
Lewis, lf	4	0	3	0
Walker, cf	3	1	1	0
Scott, ss	3	0	0	0
Thomas, c	0	0	0	0
Agnew, c	3	1	3	2
Ruth, p	0	0	0	0
Shore, p	2	1	0	0
Totals	**31**	**4**	**9**	**4**

	1	2	3		4	5	6		7	8	9		R	H	E
Wash	0	0	0		0	0	0		0	0	0		0	0	3
Bos	0	1	0		0	0	0		3	0	x		4	9	0

Washington	IP	H	R	BB	K
Ayers (L)	8	9	4	0	0

Boston	IP	H	R	BB	K
Ruth	0	0	0	1	0
Shore (W)	9	0	0	0	2

Time—1:40; Att.—16,000 (est.)

Leon Cadore
Joe Oeschger
26-Inning Game
May 1, 1920

Going the Distance, Part 1

Before there were closers, pitch counts, agents, a union, and night games in baseball, there were pitchers Leon Cadore and Joe Oeschger. They weren't just pitchers: they were warriors. Cadore was a 6'1" right-hander from Chicago who would lose more games than he won in an unspectacular 10-year major league career, but three times would pitch more than 250 innings in a season. Oeschger also was right-handed, also from Chicago, also with a losing record in a dozen big league seasons, and also a workhorse who would pitch more than 250 innings in three different seasons.

But there is more than the city of their births, undistinguished major league pitching careers, and their endurance that Cadore and Oeschger have in common. They are inextricably linked forever in baseball lore as opponents in the most remarkable game ever played.

It happened in Boston on May 1, 1920, Cadore pitching for the Brooklyn Robins, Oeschger for the home-team Braves. Just 10 days before, the two pitchers had hooked up in Brooklyn with Cadore and the Robins beating Oeschger and the Braves 1–0 in 11 innings.

A morning rain delayed the start of the game on Saturday, May 1, 1920, until 3:00 P.M. The Robins scored a run in the top of the fifth, a single by Ivy Olson driving in Ernie Krueger. The Braves tied it in the bottom of the sixth with a double by Walt Cruise and a single by Tony Boeckel.

After that, there were nothing but zeroes. A lot of zeroes. A long string of zeroes.

In the bottom of the ninth Cadore pitched out of a bases-loaded, one-out jam by getting Charley Pick to ground into an inning-ending double play. After nine innings, it was still 1–1, so they went into extra innings. Still nobody scored. And the game went on . . . and on . . . and on . . . 14 innings . . . 15. In the seventeenth, the Robins had a runner thrown out at the plate . . . and the game went on . . . 20 innings . . . 23. Into the twenty-sixth inning they went. It was now the longest game in baseball history . . . and still nobody scored.

Cadore managed to pitch out of a bases-loaded jam in the bottom of the ninth, unaware that his day was really just beginning.

> ## Into the twenty-sixth inning they went. It was now the longest game in baseball history . . . and still nobody scored.

Harold "Rowdy" Elliott replaced Krueger as Brooklyn's catcher in the seventh. Wally Hood took over in center field for the Robins in place of Hy Myers. Lloyd Christenbury pinch-hit for Mickey O'Neil in the ninth, and Hank Gowdy went in to catch for Boston. Every other starter, 15 of them including Hall of Famers Zack Wheat for Brooklyn and Rabbit Maranville for Boston, and both starting pitchers, played the entire game—all 26 innings.

When the twenty-sixth inning was concluded, umpire Barry McCormick raised his hand and signaled the game was being called because of darkness. It was 6:50 P.M., just three hours and 50 minutes after the first pitch.

Wrote the reporter for *The New York Times*:

> *McCormick remembered he had an appointment pretty soon with a succulent beefsteak. He wondered if it wasn't getting dark. He held out one hand as a test and decided that, in the gloaming, it resembled a Virginia ham. He knew it wasn't a Virginia ham, and became convinced that it was too dark to play ball.*

Players protested, none louder than Robins second baseman Olson, who begged for one more inning in an Ernie Banks–like plea. "Then we can play three games in one," Olson said.

But McCormick had made his decision. The game was recorded as a 1–1 tie.

Oeschger had lost his previous start, a foretelling 1–0, 11-inning decision to Cadore.

LEON CADORE/JOE OESCHGER 26-INNING GAME
MAY 1, 1920

Brooklyn	AB	R	H	RBI
Olson, 2b	10	0	1	1
Neis, rf	10	0	1	0
Johnston, 3b	10	0	2	0
Wheat, lf	9	0	2	0
Myers, cf	2	0	1	0
Hood, cf	6	0	1	0
Konetchy, 1b	9	0	1	0
Ward, ss	10	0	0	0
Krueger, c	2	1	0	0
Elliott, c	7	0	0	0
Cadore, p	10	0	0	0
Totals	**85**	**1**	**9**	**1**

Boston	AB	R	H	RBI
Powell, cf	7	0	1	0
Pick, 2b	11	0	0	0
Mann, lf	10	0	2	0
Cruise, rf	9	1	1	0
Holke, 1b	10	0	2	0
Boeckel, 3b	11	0	3	1
Maranville, ss	10	0	3	0
O'Neil, c	2	0	0	0
Christenbury, ph	1	0	1	0
Gowdy, c	6	0	1	0
Oeschger, p	9	0	1	0
Totals	**86**	**1**	**15**	**1**

	1 2 3	4 5 6	7 8 9	10 11 12	13 14 15	16 17 18	19 20 21	22 23 24	25 26	R H E
Br	0 0 0	0 1 0	0 0 0	0 0 0	0 0 0	0 0 0	0 0 0	0 0 0	0 0	1 9 0
Bos	0 0 0	0 0 1	0 0 0	0 0 0	0 0 0	0 0 0	0 0 0	0 0 0	0 0	1 15 0

Brooklyn	IP	H	R	ER	BB	K
Cadore	26	15	1	1	5	7

Boston	IP	H	R	ER	BB	K
Oeschger	26	9	1	1	4	7

Time—3:50; Att.—4,500

Oeschger allowed nine hits, walked four, struck out seven, and set a record for consecutive scoreless innings in one game with 21. Cadore allowed 15 hits, walked five, and struck out seven.

Nobody counted pitches in those days, but it is estimated that Cadore and Oescher each threw more than 250 pitches.

They did, however, count the number of baseballs used in the 26 innings: three.

One-Time Charley

The story of Charley Robertson, among the many stories in this book, is perhaps the most obscure, most unlikely, most unbelievable long shot. Perfect games are a shot in the dark, a game in which every single variable of the hundreds must fall exactly right. Every close pitch a strike, every Texas Leaguer an out, every hop made of candy. In Robertson's case, however, the specter of spit hangs over his deed.

The Chicago White Sox righty was making just his third major league start; he had had a cup of coffee in 1919, then was sent back to the minors. This April game against the Tigers was his second start of what was his rookie season. One clue to the future controversy is that in the time between his 1919 start and his 1922 return . . . baseball outlawed the spitball.

In front of a huge crowd of more than twenty-five thousand (the overflow was contained by ropes ringing the far reaches of the outfield forming a kind of human warning track), Robertson mowed down Tigers from start to finish. The *Chicago Daily Tribune* noted that the Sox "were not called upon to perform hair-raising feats to keep the Tygers [a play on Ty Cobb's name] away from first base. Robby was so good that ordinary fielding was all that was needed."

Cobb's Tigers had a .305 team average, the highest of any team that has fallen victim to a perfect game. Baseball historian John Thorn calls Robertson's game "perhaps the most perfect game ever pitched."

Then the muttering started. First Harry Heilman and then Cobb asked that umpire Dick Nallin inspect Robertson's pitches. Nallin said he found nothing, but did remove some balls from play. In the fifth, Cobb asked that Robertson's glove be checked. Cobb asked for more checks in the seventh, then ignominiously struck out. Finally in the ninth, Cobb made Nallin check Robertson's uniform, too.

None of it fazed the rookie, it appeared, and he got the final batter, pinch-hitter Johnny Bassler, to foul out to left. The crowd surged onto the field, carrying off their young hero. It was the ride of his life and would prove to be the only time he rose above a crowd.

The First "Perfect" Game

None of the news stories about the perfect games thrown by Cy Young, John Lee Richmond, or John M. Ward called them what we call them today. All sorts of long-winded sobriquets were used, including the exciting "no-hit, no-man-reached-first" label. But in a game story in a Chicago paper following Robertson's game, one writer noted that the "White Sox, according to captain Eddie Collins, had not let the thought of a no-hitter, to say nothing of a perfect game, dawn on them until just three men stood between Robertson and the rarest of baseball glory." Robertson's game was thus the first to be called, in contemporary reporting, "perfect."

The first coda to the game is that Cobb continued to press his case for Robertson "juicing up" the ball. He even convinced AL president Ban Johnson to investigate, but nothing came of the claim. Robertson left baseball six years later with a 49–80 career record, by far the worst of any perfect-game pitcher.

The second odd coda is Robertson's life after baseball. Unlike many one-time heroes, he essentially divorced himself from the feat and the game of baseball. After his career ended, he became a pecan farmer in Texas. A few folks tried to track him down once in a while, but without success. When Don Larsen pitched his perfect game in the 1956 World Series, many sportswriters decided to seek out the last such hurler, and they found Robertson, not hiding, but not exactly signing at card shows (or the fifties equivalent). The 34 years separating Robertson and Larsen is the longest stretch between perfect games.

He answered a few questions and then faded away again. "Baseball didn't give me a particularly bad break," he said at the time. "But I found out too late that it is ridiculous for any young man with qualifications to make good in another profession to waste time in professional athletics."

Cobb and the Tigers wish ol' Charley had stuck to pecans.

> Baseball historian John Thorn calls Robertson's game "perhaps the most perfect game ever pitched."

For one day in a career that ended with a 49–80 record, Robertson was perfect.

CHARLEY ROBERTSON'S PERFECT GAME
APRIL 30, 1922

Chicago	AB	R	H	RBI
Mulligan, ss	4	0	1	0
McClellan, 3b	3	0	1	0
Collins, 2b	3	0	1	0
Hooper, rf	3	1	0	0
Mostil, lf	4	1	1	0
Strunk, cf	3	0	0	0
Sheely, 1b	4	0	2	2
Shalk, c	4	0	1	0
Robertson, p	4	0	0	0
Totals	**32**	**2**	**7**	**2**

Detroit	AB	R	H	RBI
Blue, 1b	3	0	0	0
Cutshaw, 2b	3	0	0	0
Cobb, cf	3	0	0	0
Veach, lf	3	0	0	0
Heilmann, rf	3	0	0	0
Jones, 3b	3	0	0	0
Rigney, ss	2	0	0	0
Clark, ph	1	0	0	0
Manion, c	3	0	0	0
Pillette, p	2	0	0	0
Bassler, ph	1	0	0	0
Totals	**27**	**0**	**0**	**0**

	1	2	3	4	5	6	7	8	9	R	H	E
Chi	0	2	0	0	0	0	0	0	0	2	7	0
Det	0	0	0	0	0	0	0	0	0	0	0	1

Chicago	IP	H	R	ER	BB	K
Robertson (W)	9	0	0	0	0	6

Detroit	IP	H	R	ER	BB	K
Pillette (L)	9	7	2	2	2	5

Time—1:55; Att.—25,000 (est.)

Robertson

Stars in Their Eyes

It was the brainchild of a sportswriter.

Arch Ward of the *Chicago Tribune* conceived the idea of bringing together the greatest stars of America's new national pastime, pitting the best stars of the National League against the best of the American League in one baseball game to coincide with his city's "Century of Progress" Exposition.

The teams were selected by a poll of fans and by the two managers, John McGraw of the New York Giants for the National League, Connie Mack of the Philadelphia Athletics for the American League, and on July 6, 1933, at Chicago's Comiskey Park gathered the greatest assemblage of baseball talent ever brought together at one time (the Hall of Fame in Cooperstown was still six years in the future).

And so was born the annual Major League All-Star Game.

The big attraction was the home run, which has been credited with propelling the game to its greatest popularity. And the greatest home run hitter of them all was the mighty Babe Ruth of the New York Yankees.

"We wanted to see the Babe," said Bill Hallahan, the starting pitcher for the National League. "Sure he was old [38] and had a big waistline, but that didn't make any difference. We were on the same field with Babe Ruth."

Indeed, it was Ruth who hit the first All-Star Game home run, a two-run blast in the third inning off Hallahan that was the margin of the American League's 4–2 victory.

The home run is still the big attraction in the All-Star Game (today there is a pregame home run–hitting contest), but some of the greatest moments in All-Star history have been provided by pitchers. Perhaps the greatest came in the second game, on July 10, 1934, at New York's Polo Grounds.

The starting pitcher for the Nationals was the star of the home-team Giants, left-hander Carl Hubbell, who had won 23 games the year before. After Charlie Gehringer started the game with a single and Heinie Manush followed with a walk, Hubbell unfurled his famous screwball, or fadeaway, to strike out, in order, Ruth, Lou Gehrig, and Jimmie Foxx—the three most feared hitters in the American League.

Hubbell continued his mastery of the big American bats in the second, when he struck out Al Simmons and Joe Cronin. He had struck out five of the biggest American League stars in succession, all five of whom would eventually be elected to the Hall of Fame. Bill Dickey, another future Hall of Famer, stopped the streak with a single, but Hubbell ended the inning by striking out his pitching opponent, Lefty Gomez.

> Some of the greatest moments in All-Star history have been provided by pitchers. Perhaps the greatest came in the second game, on July 10, 1934, at New York's Polo Grounds.

For years, Hubbell's performance was the centerpiece of the annual All-Star Game, unmatched until Fernando Valenzuela of the Los Angeles Dodgers, like Hubbell a left-hander who featured a screwball, struck out five consecutive American League batters in the 57th All-Star Game in the Houston Astrodome on the night of July 15, 1986.

The game also featured the first All-Star Game appearance of Roger Clemens, who started for the American League against the New York Mets' 24-game winner, Dwight "Doc" Gooden. Clemens put on a dazzling display by facing nine National League batters and retiring them all, two by strikeout. Clemens made 24 pitches, 21 strikes, and three balls, but his performance would be overshadowed by Valenzuela.

In his first inning of work, the fourth, Valenzuela struck out Don Mattingly, Cal Ripken Jr., and Jesse Barfield. In the fifth, he struck out Lou Whitaker and Teddy Higuera to tie Hubbell, before Kirby Puckett ended the string by grounding out to shortstop Ozzie Smith.

It wasn't until 13 years later that any pitcher came close to matching Hubbell and Valenzuela. The 70th All-Star Game on the night of July 13, 1999, was a festive occasion in Boston's venerable Fenway Park. In a touching pregame ceremony, a collection of the game's greatest all-time All Stars gathered in the infield, including Boston's greatest baseball hero, Ted Williams.

The ovation for Williams was thunderous, and it continued when the ace of the Red Sox pitching staff, Pedro Martinez, took the mound to start the game for the American League.

Halfway through the regular season, Martinez already had 182 strikeouts, and he carried that theme right through this game of stars. He started the game by striking out Barry Larkin. Then he struck out the reigning National League batting champion, Larry Walker, looking. And he ended the inning by striking out Sammy Sosa, who had clouted 66 home runs the previous season.

In the second inning, Martinez faced home-run king Mark McGwire, who had belted 70 out of the park the year before, and struck him out. Martinez was one strikeout away from matching Hubbell and Valenzuela, but Matt Williams ended the streak by hitting the first pitch to second baseman Robby Alomar, who booted it for an error.

Martinez then fanned Houston slugger Jeff Bagwell, and Williams was doubled up attempting to steal second.

Martinez had faced six National League All-Star starters and struck out five of them. After two innings, Martinez's night's work was done, but not forgotten.

Hubbell stole the spotlight at the second-ever All-Star Game in 1934 by striking out five straight future Hall of Famers.

Valenzuela, also a left-handed screwballer, matched Hubbell's All-Star feat more than 50 years later.

Martinez opened the 1999 All-Star Game by fanning four straight, including two who had blasted 136 home runs the year before.

Seventeen at 17

Most kids of 17 are preparing for high school graduation, looking forward to the senior prom, deciding which college to attend, or thinking about what career they should pursue. Robert William Andrew Feller of Van Meter, Iowa, wasn't like most kids.

On September 13, 1936, 51 days before his 18th birthday, only a few days before returning to Van Meter High for his senior year, Bob Feller was pitching in the major leagues for the Cleveland Indians against the Philadelphia Athletics.

Baseball is a game played by hundreds of thousands of young Americans all across the country, a game played in huge cities and little hamlets, in organized leagues and on vacant lots.

Wherever it is played, if there is a boy with the potential to play professional baseball, major league scouts will find him. They will find him just as they found Bob Feller, at a time when scouts learned about boys with baseball talent simply by being in the right place at the right time. In 1935, the right place to be was on a wheat farm in Van Meter, population 500. Cy Slapnicka of the Cleveland Indians was there.

Bob's dad, Bill, had been a pretty good baseball player who never got beyond the local semipro ranks. When his first child came along, Bill figured here was a fine young son upon whom to build a dream.

The farm was neither large nor profitable, but there were always clothes to wear, food on the table, and a roof over their heads. And when the daily chores were done, there was always time for Bill and his son to have a catch. It was during one of those nightly catches that Bill Feller came to a decision. He had been uncertain whether to turn his son into the game's greatest shortstop or the best pitcher of all time. Bob was 11 when he rifled a throw that tore through his father's glove, striking him on the side and breaking three ribs.

"From now on, Bob," Bill Feller announced, "you're a pitcher."

Bob pitched in grade school, and in American Legion ball, then at Van Meter High, where he threw five no-hitters in his sophomore season. When the competition was inadequate for Bob's ability, his father formed his own team and built his own ballpark, clearing a field and building a diamond near the Raccoon River—his own "field of dreams."

By 1935, young Feller's reputation was statewide. He pitched for an American Legion team in Des Moines and against adults in fast semipro leagues. At 16, he pitched for the Farmers Union Insurance team of Des Moines alongside and against men almost twice his age. Enter Cy Slapnicka.

The Indians signed Feller to a contract, but a sore arm delayed his entry into professional baseball. By the summer of 1936, he was ready to pitch again, and the Indians tested him in an exhibition game at Cleveland's League Park against the famed St. Louis Cardinals' Gashouse Gang.

Feller pitched three innings in relief against the Cardinals. He faced 11 batters, allowed one hit and one walk, and struck out eight.

Thirteen days later, on July 19, 1936, the name Bob Feller appeared in a major league box score for the first time. He pitched one inning in the second game of a doubleheader against the Washington Senators, walked a man, hit a batter, struck out one, and did not allow a hit.

After a few more games in relief, Feller got his first start against the St. Louis Browns on August 23, with the Indians out of pennant contention. It was a debut that may never be matched. Certainly, it will never be forgotten. Feller, the 17-year-old wunderkind, beat the Browns 4–1, which is only part of the story. He struck out 15 Brownies, one short of the American League record, two short of the major league record, and the most strikeouts in an American League game since Bob Shawkey fanned 15 in 1919, when Feller was just a few months old.

Three starts later, Feller was matched against the Philadelphia Athletics, who were suffering through another 100-defeat season.

> When the competition was inadequate for Bob's ability, his father formed his own team and built his own ballpark, clearing a field and building a diamond near the Raccoon River—his own "field of dreams."

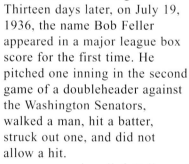

BOB FELLER
PITCHER
CLEVELAND INDIANS
Born: Van Meter, Iowa, Nov. 3, '18
Height: 6-1   Weight: 185
Bats: Right   Throws: Right
One of baseball's greatest pitchers, Bob, with the blazing fast ball, won 20 or more games for the sixth time in his career in the majors in 1951, winning 22 while losing only 8. Pitched a no-hitter in 1951, his third. Bob never played in the minors. He joined the Indians in 1936—and has been with them ever since, with the exception of three years spent in the service.

The teenage rookie relaxes after mowing down 17
Athletics in his fourth major league start.

BOB FELLER'S 17-STRIKEOUT GAME AT AGE 17
SEPTEMBER 13, 1936

Philadelphia	AB	R	H	RBI
Finney, cf	1	1	0	0
Puccinelli, rf	2	0	0	0
Moses, rf/cf	2	1	1	0
Dean, 1b	3	0	1	1
Johnson, lf	4	0	0	0
Higgins, 3b	2	0	0	0
Luby, 2b	4	0	0	0
Peters, ss	4	0	0	0
Hayes, c	4	0	0	0
Gumpert, p	3	0	0	0
Moss, ph	0	0	0	0
Totals	**29**	**2**	**2**	**1**

Cleveland	AB	R	H	RBI
Hughes, 2b	3	2	1	0
Knickerbocker, ss	2	2	1	0
Averill, cf	2	1	1	2
Trosky, 1b	4	0	2	0
Weatherly, rf	4	0	0	1
Hale, 3b	4	0	0	0
Heath, lf	3	0	1	0
George, c	4	0	1	0
Feller, p	4	0	0	0
Totals	**30**	**5**	**7**	**3**

	1	2	3	4	5	6	7	8	9	R	H	E
Phil	0	0	2	0	0	0	0	0	0	2	2	1
Cle	2	0	2	0	0	0	1	0	x	5	7	0

Philadelphia	IP	H	R	ER	BB	K
Gumpert (L)	8	7	5	NA	5	2

Cleveland	IP	H	R	ER	BB	K
Feller (W)	9	2	2	2	9	17

Time—2:03

no-hitter against the Yankees and hit a home run for the game's only score.

Against the Athletics, Feller's blazing fastball was overpowering. He struck out 17 batters, one for each year of his life, breaking the American League record of 16 set by Rube Waddell in 1908, and tying Dizzy Dean's major league record set three years before.

Before returning to Van Meter High to get his diploma, Feller would win five games and lose three in eight starts for the Indians, with five complete games and 76 strikeouts in 62 innings, all before his 18th birthday.

Despite their ineptitude as a team, the Athletics of Connie Mack were not without players of considerable ability and experience, like Wally Moses, who would bat .345 that season, .291 for a 17-year career; "Indian" Bob Johnson, who would hit 25 home runs in 1936 in the midst of a nine-year run in which he hit at least 21 home runs each year; Pinky Higgins, who would have a lifetime average of .292 for 14 seasons; and Frankie Hayes, who, 10 years later, would catch Feller's

A major leaguer at age 17, Feller and his blazing fastball became overnight sensations.

King of the Hill

Question: What is the only game in baseball history in which the batting average of one team was the same before the game and after the game?

Answer: On April 16, 1940, opening day, Bob Feller pitched a no-hitter for the Cleveland Indians against the Chicago White Sox, the first opening day no-hitter since 1909, when Leon Ames of the New York Giants no-hit the Dodgers for nine innings, but lost the game, 3–0, in the thirteenth. Feller won his game, 1–0. All White Sox players started the day batting .000 and ended the day batting .000.

"That's the game I pitched that most people talk about," Feller said. "To this day [more than 60 years later], I still look at all the box scores on opening day and if nobody has pitched a no-hitter, I say, 'Well, nobody did it again.'"

But, Feller maintains, "While that game was the most popular, it wasn't the best game I ever pitched."

Feller's best game?

April 30, 1946, at Yankee Stadium.

"Because of the opposition," Feller explained. "That was a strong Yankees team, with [Tommy] Henrich, [Charlie] Keller, and [Joe] DiMaggio. And I had just returned from the navy."

As baseball's unchallenged "King of the Hill," Feller had won 79 games and struck out 747 batters in three seasons when World War II erupted. Upon his return, skeptics wondered if Feller had lost his blazing fastball in the intervening years. When he faced the Yankees on April 30, his record was 1–2.

"I had good stuff that day, and I had a lot of confidence," Feller said. "The closest thing to a hit came on the first batter, [George] Stirnweiss, who hit a high hopper over the mound. Lou Boudreau, our shortstop, came across in front of second base, grabbed the ball barehanded, and threw the runner out at first."

For eight innings, Feller was locked in a scoreless duel with Bill Bevens, who, a year later, would come one out away from pitching the first World Series no-hitter. In the top of the ninth, Cleveland catcher Frankie Hayes belted a home run to give Feller a 1–0 lead going into the bottom of the ninth.

Stirnweiss, the first batter in the bottom of the ninth, reached on an error, and Henrich sacrificed him to second. Feller then had to face the fearsome duo of DiMaggio and Keller.

"I went to 3–2 on DiMaggio, and he fouled off about four or five pitches, then hit a ground ball to short for the second out," Feller recalled. "Keller hit a ground ball to second and that was the game."

Feller struck out 11 and walked 5.

"There were about thirty-seven thousand in the stands," he said. "At the time, it was the biggest crowd ever to see a no-hitter. Years later, Henry Kissinger told me he was there that day. He said he often went to Yankee Stadium. He'd pay 50 cents to sit in the bleachers, but on days when I pitched, he'd pay $1.10 and sit behind the Yankees dugout."

Feller won 26 games that season and struck out 348 batters, one away from the major league record at the time. He would pitch a third no-hitter against Detroit on July 1, 1951.

When he retired after the 1956 season, Feller had won 266 games, struck out 2,581 batters, and pitched three no-hitters and 12 one-hitters, leaving one to speculate how many more wins, how many more strikeouts, how many more no-hitters, and how many more one-hitters he might have had if he had not lost almost four of his most productive years serving his country.

BOB FELLER'S OPENING-DAY NO-HITTER APRIL 16, 1940

Cleveland	AB	R	H	RBI
Boudreau, ss	3	0	0	0
Weatherly, cf	4	0	1	0
Chapman, rf	3	0	0	0
Trosky, 1b	4	0	0	0
Heath, lf	4	1	1	0
Keltner, 3b	4	0	1	0
Hemsley, c	4	0	2	1
Mack, 2b	4	0	1	0
Feller, p	3	0	0	0
Totals	**33**	**1**	**6**	**1**

Chicago	AB	R	H	RBI
Kennedy, 3b	4	0	0	0
Kuhel, 1b	3	0	0	0
Kreevich, cf	3	0	0	0
Solters, lf	4	0	0	0
Appling, ss	3	0	0	0
Wright, rf	4	0	0	0
McNair, 2b	3	0	0	0
Tresh, c	2	0	0	0
Smith, p	1	0	0	0
Rosenthal, ph	1	0	0	0
Brown, p	0	0	0	0
Totals	**28**	**0**	**0**	**0**

	1	2	3	4	5	6	7	8	9	R	H	E
Cle	0	0	0	1	0	0	0	0	0	1	6	1
Chi	0	0	0	0	0	0	0	0	0	0	0	1

Cleveland	IP	H	R	ER	BB	K
Feller (W)	9	0	0	0	5	8

Chicago	IP	H	R	ER	BB	K
Smith (L)	8	6	1	1	2	5
Brown	1	0	0	0	0	0

Time—2:24; Att.—14,000 (est.)

Twice Upon a Time

An overflow crowd of 38,748 filed excitedly into Brooklyn's Ebbets Field on June 15, 1938, for a game between the home team Dodgers and the Cincinnati Reds. They had been lured as witnesses to history, the first night game ever played in the venerable ballpark. Little did they know that they would be witnesses to baseball history of another sort.

Pitching for Cincinnati would be Johnny Vander Meer, a 23-year-old left-hander who just four days earlier had pitched a no-hitter against the Boston Bees (the once and future Boston Braves), which was enough to attract the curiosity seekers and baseball aficionados in the crowd.

When he was 17 and still had not thrown a baseball as a professional, Vander Meer was selected to appear in a documentary film commissioned by the National League about a typical American boy getting his first tryout with a major league team. The purpose of the film was to entice boys into a career in baseball.

"Find me a lad who has a modest background," National League president John Heydler instructed Dave Driscoll, the business manager of the Brooklyn Dodgers, who was charged with locating a boy to be the subject of the film. "His people must be middle class, he must be clean-cut, religious, and his father should have an industrial background."

Driscoll found John Samuel Vander Meer about 25 miles from Brooklyn, in Midland Park, New Jersey, the son of a stone mason who had come to the United States from Holland. Young Vander Meer was a left-handed fireballer who pitched in a local church league.

For Driscoll and the Dodgers, as well as for young Vander Meer, it presented an ideal opportunity. The boy would go to the Dodgers' spring training camp in Miami to film the picture, and at the same time, the Dodgers could evaluate him as a prospect.

Dodgers manager Max Carey was less than impressed with the erratic left-hander and decided to send him home without a contract when the film was completed. Joe Shaute, a veteran left-handed pitcher who had taken a liking to the boy, interceded, pleading with Carey to give the kid a chance. The manager agreed to sign him and send him to Dayton, a Dodgers farm team in Ohio. There Vander Meer won 11 games and lost 10, a record that indicated enough promise to warrant another chance. However, Dayton manager Ducky Holmes thought the kid was too wild and recommended that Vander Meer be released.

Unbreakable?

Almost 70 years have passed since Johnny Vander Meer pitched back-to-back no-hitters, and except for Ewell Blackwell nine years later, no pitcher has come close to duplicating the feat. It remains one baseball record that likely will never be broken, for in order to *break* Vander Meer's record, a pitcher would have to pitch *three* consecutive no-hitters.

Confused and discouraged, the young man returned to New Jersey, but soon learned he had been purchased by Scranton. This was even more confusing because Scranton was in a higher minor league classification than Dayton. It wasn't until he arrived in Scranton that the mystery was solved. On the club was his old friend, Joe Shaute, who had been sold by Brooklyn to Cincinnati, and then farmed out to Scranton.

Once again, Shaute took Vander Meer under his wing, and with the veteran's tutelage, Vander Meer's progress was so encouraging that Larry MacPhail, general manager of the Cincinnati Reds, purchased his contract for $4,000.

> His next start would be on June 15 in Brooklyn, where the main attraction was the rare spectacle of baseball after dark, an experiment that had been introduced by Larry MacPhail three years earlier in Cincinnati.

After an average year in Scranton, Vander Meer's contract was sold to Boston. But MacPhail's interest was renewed when the young left-hander struck out 295 batters at Durham in 1936 and was named Minor League Player of the Year. This time it cost MacPhail $10,000 to get Vander Meer back to Cincinnati.

At Syracuse in 1937, Vandy won only 5 games and lost 11. But Cincinnati manager Bill McKechnie called him up to the Reds late in the season, and he posted a 3–5 record. The manager liked what he saw of the kid enough to put him in his starting rotation the next season. A month into the season, McKechnie's confidence in the rookie left-hander was rewarded when Vander Meer shut out the New York Giants at the Polo Grounds.

Three weeks later, on June 11, Vander Meer faced the Boston Bees. He was particularly fast that day. He fired his high hard one past Boston hitters, and in nine innings, not one of them could hit him safely. Johnny Vander Meer had pitched a no-hitter in his rookie season.

JOHNNY VANDER MEER'S CONSECUTIVE NO-HITTERS, GAME 1
JUNE 11, 1938

Boston	AB	R	H	RBI
Moore, rf	1	0	0	0
Fletcher, 1b	1	0	0	0
Mueller, ph	1	0	0	0
Cooney, 1b/rf	3	0	0	0
V. DiMaggio, cf	2	0	0	0
Cuccinello, 2b	2	0	0	0
Reis, lf	3	0	0	0
English, 3b	2	0	0	0
Riddle, c	3	0	0	0
Warstler, ss	2	0	0	0
Kahle, ph	1	0	0	0
MacFayden, p	2	0	0	0
Maggert, ph	1	0	0	0
Totals	**24**	**0**	**0**	**0**

Cincinnati	AB	R	H	RBI
Frey, 2b	4	0	0	0
Berger, lf	3	2	1	0
Goodman, rf	3	0	0	1
McCormick, 1b	4	0	1	0
Lombardi, c	4	1	2	2
Craft, cf	3	0	0	0
Riggs, 3b	3	0	1	0
Myers, ss	3	0	0	0
Vander Meer, p	3	0	1	0
Totals	**30**	**3**	**6**	**3**

	1	2	3	4	5	6	7	8	9	R	H	E
Bos	0	0	0	0	0	0	0	0	0	0	0	0
Cin	0	0	0	1	0	2	0	0	x	3	6	1

Boston	IP	H	R	ER	BB	K
MacFayden (L)	8	6	3	3	1	4

Cincinnati	IP	H	R	ER	BB	K
Vander Meer (W)	9	0	0	0	3	4

Time—1:48

It's safe to say that Vander Meer was in command of his pitches during one historic stretch in 1938.

CHAPTER 13

The first night game at Brooklyn's Ebbets Field was the site of Vander Meer's second consecutive no-hitter.

His next start would be on June 15 in Brooklyn, where the main attraction was the rare spectacle of baseball after dark, an experiment that had been introduced by Larry MacPhail three years earlier in Cincinnati. When the energetic and imaginative MacPhail moved to Brooklyn, he took his midsummer night's dream with him.

By the fourth inning, fans had adjusted to the novelty of night baseball with the field illuminated by bright lights, and they turned their attention to Vander Meer, who had not allowed a hit.

Until 1938, seven pitchers had thrown two no-hitters, but none had ever pitched two in one season, let alone in successive starts. Baseball experts contended that a no-hitter was such a psychological and emotional drain that it often took a pitcher three or four starts for him to build up to a psychological peak again.

Vander Meer was a rookie who never heard of this theory. He simply kept mowing the Dodgers down and moved into the ninth inning with a 6–0 lead, his no-hitter still intact. The first batter in the bottom of the ninth was veteran first baseman Buddy Hassett, who swung at the first pitch and sent a bouncer to the first base side of the pitcher's mound. Vander Meer swept off the mound, scooped up the ball with his glove hand, and, in one continuous motion, tagged Hassett as he sped by.

The partisan Brooklyn fans, mixed with many of Vander Meer's friends and relatives from nearby New Jersey, moaned when Vander Meer walked the next two batters, Babe Phelps and Cookie Lavagetto, bringing up Brooklyn's most feared slugger, Dolph Camilli, who also walked, filling the bases.

Ernie Koy was the next batter and Vander Meer poured in a strike. The next pitch was hit on the ground to third. Lew Riggs fielded it, took his time, and fired home for the second out. There was no time for catcher Ernie Lombardi to double Koy at first.

The bases remained loaded for the next hitter, Leo Durocher, a fierce competitor known as a dangerous hitter in the clutch. Vander Meer threw a ball, then a strike, then another strike. Durocher swung viciously at the next pitch, and the crowd groaned as the ball soared on a sharp line into the right field corner: there was a sigh of relief as the ball hooked foul.

Vandy reared back and put everything he had into the next pitch. Durocher swung and lifted a high, lazy fly to center field. Harry Craft moved in and caught the ball easily, and Johnny Vander Meer had made baseball history. He had completed baseball's first back-to-back no-hitters, and he had spoiled Brooklyn's first night game for Larry MacPhail, who had twice purchased Vander Meer's contract in Cincinnati.

A series of arm problems hampered Vander Meer's career. Two years after he had reached baseball's summit, he was sent to the minor leagues. He returned to Cincinnati for a brief run of success, winning 49 games from 1941 to 1943. After two bad years, he came back to win 17 in 1948. But two years later, he was traded to the Chicago Cubs, and then to the Cleveland Indians. He finished his career with a record of 119–121, and never came close to being the pitcher he was in 1938.

Vander Meer finally did pitch a third no-hitter in 1952, but he pitched it for Tulsa in the Texas League against Beaumont, which was managed by Harry Craft, the Reds center fielder who had caught Leo Durocher's fly ball for the last out on Vander Meer's greatest day 14 years earlier.

JOHNNY VANDER MEER'S CONSECUTIVE NO-HITTERS, GAME 2
JUNE 15, 1938

Brooklyn	AB	R	H	RBI
Cuyler, rf	2	0	0	0
Coscarart, 2b	2	0	0	0
Brack, ph	1	0	0	0
Hudson, 2b	1	0	0	0
Hassett, lf	4	0	0	0
Phelps, c	3	0	0	0
Rosen, pr	0	0	0	0
Lavagetto, 3b	2	0	0	0
Camilli, 1b	1	0	0	0
Koy, cf	4	0	0	0
Durocher, ss	4	0	0	0
Butcher, p	0	0	0	0
Pressnell, p	2	0	0	0
Hamlin, p	0	0	0	0
English, ph	0	0	0	0
Tamulis, p	0	0	0	0
Totals	**27**	**0**	**0**	**0**

Cincinnati	AB	R	H	RBI
Frey, 2b	5	0	1	0
Berger, lf	5	1	3	1
Goodman, rf	3	2	1	0
McCormick, 1b	5	1	1	3
Lombardi, c	5	1	1	0
Craft, cf	5	0	3	1
Riggs, 3b	4	0	1	1
Myers, ss	4	0	0	0
Vander Meer, p	4	1	1	0
Totals	**38**	**6**	**11**	**6**

	1	2	3	4	5	6	7	8	9		R	H	E
Br	0	0	0	0	0	0	0	0	0		0	0	2
Cin	0	0	4	0	0	0	1	1	x		6	11	0

Brooklyn	IP	H	R	ER	BB	K
Butcher (L)	2.2	5	4	3	3	1
Pressnell	3.1	3	0	0	0	3
Hamlin	2	3	2	2	1	3
Tamulis	1	0	0	0	0	1

Cincinnati	IP	H	R	ER	BB	K
Vander Meer (W)	9	0	0	0	8	7

Time—2:23; Att.—38,748

PART II

The Golden Age

1946 to 1968

Jim Kaat's Top 20 Pitchers of All Time

1. Sandy Koufax
2. Walter Johnson
3. Bob Feller
4. Warren Spahn
5. Bob Gibson
6. Steve Carlton
7. Tom Seaver
8. Lefty Grove
9. Juan Marichal
10. Christy Mathewson
11. Roger Clemens
12. Greg Maddux
13. Ferguson Jenkins
14. Jim Palmer
15. Grover Cleveland Alexander
16. Catfish Hunter
17. Robin Roberts
18. Whitey Ford
19. Randy Johnson
20. Nolan Ryan

Jerome Holtzman's Top 20 Pitchers of All Time

1. Sandy Koufax
2. Lefty Grove
3. Greg Maddux
4. Roger Clemens
5. Walter Johnson
6. Bob Gibson
7. Warren Spahn
8. Bob Feller
9. Smokey Joe Wood
10. Carl Hubbell
11. Grover Cleveland Alexander
12. Tom Seaver
13. Christy Mathewson
14. Steve Carlton
15. Nolan Ryan
16. Randy Johnson
17. Charley Radbourn
18. Cy Young
19. Juan Marichal
20. Jim Palmer

Unleashing the Whip

Word of Johnny Vander Meer's second consecutive no-hitter in Brooklyn on June 15, 1938, spread like wildfire across the country, reaching all the way to the little town of San Dimas, California, some three thousand miles away, where a tall, skinny right-handed pitcher for Bonita High School was attracting professional baseball scouts. Ewell Blackwell, a gangling 6'5" pitcher, possessed a devastating sidearm motion. On the same team was an outfielder who also was attracting attention, but in another sport. His name was Glenn Davis, and he would go on to West Point to win fame as Mr. Outside to Doc Blanchard's Mr. Inside, possibly the greatest one-two running punch in college football history.

When Blackwell graduated, the Dodgers offered him a contract. Blackie was interested, but only if the Dodgers would permit him to go to spring training with the big team. The Dodgers refused, and Blackwell passed up professional baseball to enroll in California's LaVerne Teachers College on a basketball scholarship.

Along came the Cincinnati Reds with another contract offer. Again Blackwell repeated his request to be allowed to go to spring training. This time, Cincinnati agreed, and Blackwell signed with the Reds' farm team in Ogden, Utah. Blackwell never saw Ogden. As he had planned, the Reds were so impressed with him during the spring of 1942, they decided to keep him in the major leagues.

It was soon obvious that the 19-year-old with no professional experience was in over his head. The Reds sent Blackwell to Syracuse, where he gained the needed experience and terrorized International League batters, winning 16 games during the regular season. In the playoffs, he won four games and chalked up 30 consecutive scoreless innings before an attack of pneumonia sidelined him for the Little World Series.

World War II interrupted Blackie's career for the next three seasons, but he returned to Cincinnati in 1946. Late arriving to spring training and out of competition for three years, he managed only a 9–13 record. He nevertheless impressed National League opponents, especially the right-handed hitters, with his intimidating sidearm deliveries. They nicknamed him "the Whip" because of the whip-like motion he achieved when he brought his long, dangling arm around by way of third base.

"He pitches like a man falling out of a tree," said the veteran Dodgers shortstop, Pee Wee Reese.

By 1947 Blackwell was ready to win in the big leagues. He started slowly, posting a 2–2 record in the first month of the season, but as he faced the Boston Braves on the night of June 18, he had reeled off seven consecutive victories. Number eight was a classic. He set the Braves down without a hit.

Ever since Vander Meer pitched consecutive no-hitters nine years earlier, interest heightened whenever a pitcher went to the mound in his first start after pitching a no-hitter. Since Vandy, there had been nine no-hitters in the big leagues, but not one pitcher was able to come close to doubling up. Now Blackwell was the 10th to try.

In this case, the background for his attempt was marked by several startling coincidences. Both Vander Meer and Blackwell pitched for the Cincinnati Reds. Vander Meer's two no-hitters had come in the month of June, nine years earlier; Blackwell's no-hitter was on June 18, and his next start would be four days later in Cincinnati. Finally, Vander Meer's first no-hitter came against Boston and his second against the Dodgers. Blackwell pitched his no-hitter against Boston and would try for his second straight against . . . the Dodgers.

A capacity crowd of 31,204 filled Cincinnati's Crosley Field on the afternoon of Sunday, June 22, 1947. It was the first game of a doubleheader, and the fans had come mainly to see if Blackwell could make baseball lightning strike twice.

Vander Meer was still a member of the Reds and his voice was the loudest as he leaned on the top step of the dugout shouting encouragement as Blackwell calmly and effectively set the Dodgers down in the early innings.

Through seven innings, Blackwell clung to a 1–0 lead and thrilled the crowd as he turned the Dodgers back without a hit. In the last of the eighth, the Reds scored three times, putting the game out of reach for the Dodgers.

The Dodgers' first batter in the ninth was Gene Hermanski, pinch-hitting for pitcher Hank Behrman. He hit a short fly to left field, an easy chance for Augie Galan.

That brought up Eddie Stanky, the tough little competitor known as "the Brat" because he antagonized opponents with his peskiness at bat and in the field. Stanky took the first pitch. On the second, he rifled a smash through the center of the diamond. Because of his octopus-like wind-up

> It was the first game of a doubleheader and the fans had come mainly to see if Blackwell could make baseball lightning strike twice.

It was another lanky Cincinnati Reds pitcher, Ewell Blackwell in 1947, who nearly duplicated Vander Meer's remarkable feat.

Blackwell, also known as "the Whip," celebrates after his first masterpiece against Boston.

EWELL BLACKWELL'S NO-HITTER
JUNE 18, 1947

Boston	AB	R	H	RBI
Holmes, rf	3	0	0	0
Hopp, cf	2	0	0	0
Rowell, lf	4	0	0	0
Elliott, 3b	3	0	0	0
Torgeson, 1b	3	0	0	0
Masi, c	2	0	0	0
Sisti, ss	2	0	0	0
Ryan, 2b	3	0	0	0
Wright, p	0	0	0	0
Lanfranconi, p	2	0	0	0
McCormick, ph	1	0	0	0
Karl, p	0	0	0	0
Totals	**25**	**0**	**0**	**0**

Cincinnati	AB	R	H	RBI
Baumholtz, rf	5	2	4	0
Zientara, 2b	3	0	1	0
Hatton, 3b	1	2	1	0
Young, 1b	5	2	2	6
Haas, cf	4	0	0	0
Galan, lf	5	0	2	0
Miller, ss	5	0	0	0
Lamanno, c	3	0	1	0
Blackwell, p	4	0	1	0
Totals	**35**	**6**	**12**	**6**

	1	2	3	4	5	6	7	8	9	R	H	E
Bos	0	0	0	0	0	0	0	0	0	0	0	2
Cin	3	0	0	0	0	0	0	3	x	6	12	0

Boston	IP	H	R	ER	BB	K
Wright (L)	1.1	3	3	NA	1	1
Lanfranconi	5.2	6	0	0	1	0
Karl	1.0	3	3	NA	1	0

Cincinnati	IP	H	R	ER	BB	K
Blackwell (W)	9	0	0	0	4	3

If I was quicker, I would have. And if I got that one, Robinson never would have come to bat and I would have had my no-hitter. I have only myself to blame."

Blackwell finished the 1947 season with a record of 22–8, but arm injuries and the removal of a kidney hampered him for the remainder of his career, which ended in 1955 after he had pitched in two games for the Kansas City Athletics. In 10 big league seasons, Blackwell won 82 games, more than a quarter of them in one memorable season.

and awkward follow-through, Blackwell never was in good position to field a ball. This time, it was his undoing.

He reached down with his glove for Stanky's smash, but he was not fast enough, and the ball squirted through his legs, bounced over second base, and trickled into center field as second baseman Benny Zientara and shortstop Eddie Miller tried vainly to flag it down. It was a hit, clean and unquestioned, and it prevented Blackwell from joining Vander Meer's exclusive club.

One out later, Jackie Robinson also singled, which took a little of the sting out of Blackwell's failure . . . but only a little.

"It was my own fault I didn't get it," Blackwell said to sportswriters gathered around his locker after the game. "I should have fielded Stanky's ball.

EWELL BLACKWELL
PITCHER
CINCINNATI REDS

Born: Fresno, Calif., Oct. 23, 1922
Height: 6-6   Weight: 195
Bats: Right   Throws: Right

One of the best pitchers in baseball, the string-bean right hander has been plagued by illness the last few seasons. He appeared in 38 games for the Reds in 1951, winning 16 and losing 15. His earned run average was 3.44. Pitched a no-hitter against Boston in 1947. Won 22 games in 1947 to lead the league. Has been with the Reds since 1942, although he spent three years in service.

(CUT ALONG THIS LINE)

1952 RED MAN ALL-STAR TEAM
NATIONAL LEAGUE SERIES—PLAYER #3

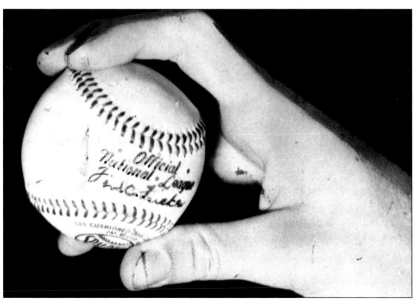

BLACKWELL'S ATTEMPTED SECOND NO-HITTER JUNE 22, 1947

Brooklyn	AB	R	H	RBI
Stanky, 2b	4	0	1	0
Gionfriddo, lf	4	0	0	0
Robinson, 1b	4	0	1	0
Furillo, cf	3	0	0	0
Walker, rf	1	0	0	0
Jorgensen, 3b	3	0	0	0
Reese, ss	2	0	0	0
Vaughan, ph	1	0	0	0
Rojek, ss	0	0	0	0
Hodges, c	2	0	0	0
Snider, ph	1	0	0	0
Bragan, c	0	0	0	0
Hatten, p	2	0	0	0
Behrman, p	0	0	0	0
Hermanski, ph	1	0	0	0
Totals	**28**	**0**	**2**	**0**

Cincinnati	AB	R	H	RBI
Baumholtz, rf	2	0	0	0
Zientara, 2b	4	0	0	0
Hatton, 3b	4	2	1	0
Haas, cf	3	1	1	0
Young, 1b	2	0	0	0
Galan, lf	2	1	0	1
Miller, ss	4	0	2	3
Lamanno, c	2	0	0	0
Blackwell, p	4	0	0	0
Totals	**27**	**4**	**4**	**4**

	1	2	3	4	5	6	7	8	9	R	H	E
Br	0	0	0	0	0	0	0	0	0	0	2	0
Cin	0	0	0	0	0	1	0	3	x	4	4	0

Brooklyn	IP	H	R	ER	BB	K
Hatten (L)	5.2	1	1	1	6	2
Behrman	2.1	3	3	3	3	1

Cincinnati	IP	H	R	ER	BB	K
Blackwell (W)	9	2	0	0	3	6

Time—2:13; Att.—31,204

EWELL BLACKWELL

Allie Oops

Shadows fall quickly on Yankee Stadium in the autumn of the year, making high fly balls difficult to catch. Many a player's career has been tarnished by an inability to become accustomed to the lengthening shadows during day games in September and October.

As Yogi Berra once said, "It gets late early out there."

On September 28, 1951, a typical sunny autumn afternoon at New York, the New York Yankees faced the Boston Red Sox in a doubleheader in Yankee Stadium. The huge ballpark was splashed with bright sunshine as the first game started. By the seventh inning, the entire infield and most of the outfield were darkened by shadows.

New York's ace pitcher, Allie Reynolds, affectionately known as the "Chief" because he was part Creek Indian, was pitching for the home side. Reynolds had come to the Yankees before the 1947 season in a much ballyhooed, often criticized trade with the Cleveland Indians.

Reynolds had been a mediocre pitcher with Cleveland, posting a record of 51–47 in four seasons when the Yankees got him in exchange for veteran second baseman Joe Gordon, a perennial All-Star and the American League's Most Valuable Player in 1942. Given their choice of Reynolds or Steve Gromek, Yankees management solicited their star, Joe DiMaggio, for his opinion.

"Reynolds is the one I'd take," said DiMaggio. "He can buzz the high, hard one by me any time he has a mind to."

That was good enough for the Yankees. If the great Yankee Clipper had trouble hitting against Reynolds, he figured to be tough on most batters.

Reynolds was an instant success in New York. In his first year with the Yankees, he won 19 games and followed that up with 16, 17, and 16 wins. Now, late in the 1951 season, he was on his way to another successful season.

Earlier that year, on July 12, Reynolds had pitched a no-hitter against his old team, the Indians, in a thrilling 1–0 duel with the great Bob Feller, just 11 days after Feller had pitched the third no-hitter of his illustrious career. Feller had allowed the Yankees just four hits, one of them a seventh-inning home run by another former Indian, Gene Woodling.

> **Earlier that year, Reynolds had pitched a no-hitter against his old team, the Indians, in a thrilling 1–0 duel with the great Bob Feller, just 11 days after Feller had pitched the third no-hitter of his illustrious career.**

Now, on September 28, Reynolds was flirting with history once more. As he strode to the mound for the ninth inning, he had not allowed a hit to the powerhouse Red Sox, a team with a potent lineup that included Dominic DiMaggio, Johnny Pesky, Bobby Doerr, Walt Dropo, Vern Stephens, and the incomparable Ted Williams. Reynolds was three outs away from becoming the first pitcher to pitch two no-hitters in one season since Johnny Vander Meer did it in consecutive games 13 years earlier.

Reynolds' bid for a second no-hitter was a bonus in a doubleheader that already had huge significance for the fans. If the Yankees won both games, they would clinch their third straight American League pennant. But now, with the Yankees leading 8–0, it was the potential of a no-hitter that had the fans enthralled.

Reynolds disposed of the first two Red Sox in the top of the ninth. Now he would have to face the redoubtable Williams, widely acclaimed as the greatest hitter the game has known. Despite missing three years during World War II, Williams had won four batting titles, had a lifetime average over .340, and was the last man to bat over .400—hitting .406 in 1941.

Although 1951 was not one of his better seasons, he was still a formidable threat and a feared hitter at age 33. He would finish the season second in the league in home runs with 30, second in RBIs with 126, and fourth in batting at .318.

Quickly, Reynolds buzzed two strikes over the plate with a blazing fastball, his trademark. Now the Chief was one strike away as he delivered his next pitch. The fastball was a blur, but Williams swung and got a piece of the ball, sending a high, twisting pop fly behind home plate. Yogi Berra eagerly tore off his mask, flung it a safe distance away from home plate, and dashed back, looking up and trying to find the ball in the shadows.

The ball was twisting crazily as it fell. At the last moment, Berra lunged and the ball hit his mitt, but he was off balance and the ball popped out of the mitt and plunked to the ground.

"I wanted to crawl into a hole," Berra said later.

Instead, he sheepishly went to the mound, but before Berra could say a word, Reynolds gave him a pat on the back and told him to forget it.

It's dangerous to give a hitter a second chance, especially a hitter of Williams' skill and stature.

ALLIE REYNOLDS' SECOND NO-HITTER
SEPTEMBER 28, 1951

Boston	AB	R	H	RBI
D. DiMaggio, cf	2	0	0	0
Pesky, 2b	4	0	0	0
Williams, lf	3	0	0	0
Vollmer, rf	2	0	0	0
Goodman, 1b	3	0	0	0
Boudreau, ss	3	0	0	0
Hatfield, 3b	3	0	0	0
Robinson, c	3	0	0	0
Parnell, p	1	0	0	0
Scarborough, p	1	0	0	0
Taylor, p	0	0	0	0
Maxwell, ph	1	0	0	0
Totals	**26**	**0**	**0**	**0**

New York	AB	R	H	RBI
Rizzuto, ss	5	1	1	0
Coleman, 2b	3	2	1	1
Bauer, rf	4	0	1	1
J. DiMaggio, cf	4	0	1	0
McDougald, 3b	3	1	1	1
Berra, c	4	0	1	1
Woodling, lf	4	2	2	1
Collins, 1b	4	2	2	2
Reynolds, p	3	0	0	0
Totals	**34**	**8**	**10**	**7**

	1	2	3	4	5	6	7	8	9	R	H	E
Bos	0	0	0	0	0	0	0	0	0	0	0	3
NYY	2	0	2	1	0	2		0	1	x	8	10	1

Boston	IP	H	R	ER	BB	K
Parnell (L)	3	5	5	NA	2	2
Scarborough	3	3	2	NA	0	0
Taylor	2	2	1	NA	0	0

New York	IP	H	R	ER	BB	K
Reynolds (W)	9	0	0	0	4	9

Time—2:12; Att.—39,038

Reynolds pitched again . . . another fastball . . . and again Williams sent a high, twisting foul behind home plate. "Déjà vu all over again," as Berra would say. Again Berra tossed his mask and planted his feet firmly, waiting the ball to descend. He picked the ball out of the shadows as it hurtled down and plopped right in the pocket of his mitt.

Berra did not muff his second chance. He squeezed the ball and then leaped into the air and dashed to the mound to embrace Allie Reynolds, who had pitched his second no-hitter in 10 weeks.

CHAPTER 15

Reynolds savors the moment in the Yankee Stadium clubhouse after his second no-hitter of the 1951 season.

Bill Veeck's Bonus Bobo

A no-hitter is one of the rarest feats in sports. Since the start of baseball's "modern era" in 1901, more than 163,000 games have been played in the major leagues. In that time there have been 209 games pitched that met the criteria for a no-hitter set forth by Major League Baseball (the number does not include no-hitters by more than one pitcher), or approximately one no-hitter for every 780 games. The odds against a pitcher throwing a no-hitter, therefore, are about 1,560 to 1, because, in every game, there are two pitchers with a chance to pitch a no-hitter.

There is no restriction on who can pitch a no-hitter. Everybody starts from scratch, no previous experience required, and no résumé needed. Ernie Koob pitched one, and he won only 23 major league games. Bob Groom, who lost a record 19 straight games as a rookie in 1909, pitched a no-hitter in 1917, the year he led the American League in defeats for the second time with 19. But Grover Cleveland Alexander never pitched a no-hitter, and he won 373 major league games. Lefty Grove, a 300-game winner, did not pitch one, but Bill McCahan, who won only 16 games, did.

While a no-hitter gives a man a measure of immortality, it does not guarantee him permanent employment. In the nine years from 1958 through 1966, there were 21 no-hitters pitched by 16 different pitchers, and 14 of them were traded and told to be immortals somewhere else.

Neither Eddie Plank nor Early Wynn nor Whitey Ford, who combined for 863 wins and are all in the Hall of Fame, ever pitched a no-hitter. Cliff Chambers, Ed Head, and Bob Keegan, who combined for 115 wins, all did. Dizzy Dean, who won 30 games in one season, never pitched a no-hitter. Neither did Robin Roberts, who started 609 major league games. And then there was Bobo Holloman.

By the time he reached the major leagues with the St. Louis Browns in 1953, Alva "Bobo" Holloman had spent nearly a decade in the minor leagues. In 1952 he had a record of 16–7 for Syracuse of the International League, and then followed it up by winning two games in the Puerto Rico Winter League World Series. That caught the attention of Bill Veeck, the legendary baseball impresario and maverick one-legged owner of the pathetic Browns. Always on the lookout for a gate attraction—and a bargain—Veeck rolled the dice with Bobo. The price was cheap enough

for the cash-strapped Veeck—$10,000 plus an additional $25,000 if Holloman survived the June 15 deadline for trimming team rosters.

Veeck was a good judge of baseball talent, but he had never seen Holloman pitch. Still, the reports were good and his record was, too, so Veeck figured Bobo had to be worth a $10,000 gamble. He was never so wrong in his life.

To put it politely, Bobo was something of a character. When the Browns purchased his contract, they sent him a publicity questionnaire—routine procedure with most teams when they acquire a new player. One of the questions was: "Do you have any superstitions?"

"Yeah," replied Holloman. "I write the initials of my wife and kid in the foul lines before I pitch. ALWAYS." The capital letters were Bobo's.

One look at his new pitcher and it became obvious to Veeck that he had made a terrible mistake. Survive the June 15 deadline? Bobo would be lucky if he survived batting practice.

"He could outtalk me, outcon me, and outpester me," wrote Veeck in his book, *Veeck as in Wreck*, "but he couldn't outpitch me. In spring training he was hit harder trying to get batters out than our batting practice pitchers who were trying to let them hit."

One thing consoled Veeck. There was no way Holloman would survive past the June 15 deadline, and Veeck would save $25,000.

When the season started, Bobo was used in a few mop-up relief assignments by manager Marty Marion with the expected results.

"I'm a starting pitcher, not a relief pitcher," Holloman protested. "Give me a starting shot and I'll show you what I can do."

Holloman pestered Marion every day for a month, and when his blathering got him nowhere, he took his case to Veeck, who listened with a sympathetic ear. Finally Veeck told Marion to let Holloman have his shot. What better way to dispose of him once and for all?

Bobo was named to start against the powerful New York Yankees, which Veeck knew was tantamount to tossing a side of beef to a pride of hungry lions. As Bobo was about to deliver his first pitch to Yankees leadoff batter Phil Rizzuto, there was a cloudburst, and a rainstorm forced cancellation of the game.

Perhaps Veeck felt sorry for poor Bobo because his next start, on May 6, was against the pathetic Philadelphia Athletics, the softest competition in

> While a no-hitter gives a man a measure of immortality, it does not guarantee him permanent employment. In the nine years from 1958 through 1966, there were 21 no-hitters pitched by 16 different pitchers, and 14 of them were traded and told to be immortals somewhere else.

Holloman, one of the more unlikely members of the elite no-hitter club, is congratulated by St. Louis Browns teammates in 1953.

BOBO HOLLOMAN'S NO-HITTER
MAY 6, 1953

Philadelphia	AB	R	H	RBI
Joost, ss	3	0	0	0
Philley, cf	4	0	0	0
Babe, 3b	3	0	0	0
Robinson, 1b	4	0	0	0
Clark, rf	3	0	0	0
Zernial, lf	3	0	0	0
Michaels, 2b	3	0	0	0
Astroth, c	1	0	0	0
Martin, p	1	0	0	0
Hamilton, ph	1	0	0	0
Scheib, p	0	0	0	0
Valo, ph	0	0	0	0
DeMaestri, pr	0	0	0	0
Totals	**26**	**0**	**0**	**0**

St. Louis	AB	R	H	RBI
Groth, cf	5	0	2	1
Hunter, ss	5	1	2	0
Dyck, lf	3	1	1	1
Elliott, 3b	4	0	2	0
Wertz, rf	3	0	1	1
Moss, c	5	2	2	0
Sievers, 1b	3	1	1	0
Young, 2b	2	1	0	0
Holloman, p	3	0	2	3
Totals	**33**	**6**	**13**	**6**

	1	2	3	4	5	6	7	8	9	R	H	E
Phil	0	0	0	0	0	0	0	0	0	0	0	1
StL	0	1	1	0	1	1	2	0	x	6	13	1

Philadelphia	IP	H	R	ER	BB	K
Martin (L)	5	7	3	2	4	2
Scheib	3	6	3	3	3	1

St. Louis	IP	H	R	ER	BB	K
Holloman (W)	9	0	0	0	5	3

Time—2:09; Att.—2,473

the American League. Bobo etched an *N* for Nan and a *G* for Gary near the foul line and went out to pitch. Again, there was a cloudburst, but the intermittent rain was not heavy enough to call the game.

Everything Bobo threw was belted, and everywhere the ball went, there was a Brownie to catch it. It was miraculous. Billy Hunter was an acrobat at shortstop. Jim Dyck spent most of the night climbing the left field wall to pull down long drives. Roy Sievers made three incredible plays at first base.

Because the night was hot and humid and the air was damp and heavy, drives that would normally soar out of the park were held up and caught at the fences. And just when Bobo appeared to be tiring and running out of gas, a shower would sweep across the field and delay the game long enough for him to rest and come back refreshed.

It went on like this for nine unbelievable innings: fantastic catches, drives curving foul at the last moment, hard shots hit right into fielders' gloves. And when it was over, Bobo Holloman had a no-hitter, and Bill Veeck had an expensive problem.

Bobo had become the first pitcher in baseball's modern era to pitch a no-hitter in his first major league start. Suddenly, he was an immortal, and not even Bill Veeck would dream of sending an immortal to the minor leagues. He was stuck with him past the June 15 deadline.

Holloman's no-hitter was the first for the Browns in 36 years, to the day. It was also the last no-hitter pitched for the St. Louis Browns. The following year, they moved out of St. Louis and became the Baltimore Orioles. When they did, Bobo Holloman was not around to make the move with them.

He made nine more starts and somehow managed to win two more games, but he never pitched another complete game. On July 23, Bobo was sold to Toronto of the International League, never again to be heard from in the major leagues. The price for Bobo's contract was $7,500, representing a loss of $27,500 for Bill Veeck.

Holloman

One for the Ages

When counting years, we divide all of time into two eras: B.C. and A.D.

When looking at perfect games, the division is thus: B.L. and A.L. (and we don't mean American League).

Before Don Larsen threw his perfect game in the fifth game of the 1956 World Series, perfect games were, well, not that big a deal. They were an odd anomaly, briefly celebrated and then glossed over. Those were the bad old days B.L.—Before Larsen.

After Larsen did what many thought impossible (and, in fact, no one has repeated the feat in the Series since), perfect games leapt light-years ahead in their appeal, estimation, and interest among baseball fans and players. Welcome to A.L.—After Larsen. The impact on Larsen has been well-documented: the performance simply changed his life forever (though it didn't help him finish his career with a winning record). The impact on the importance and relevance of perfect games underwent an even more tectonic change.

As season after season goes by and no one even approaches a no-hitter in the postseason, let alone a perfecto, Larsen's feat—and with it, the feat of perfection—simply rises in appeal.

Of course, writing about Larsen's perfect game is like writing about the sunset: everyone has seen one and everyone knows what happens, it's just a matter of your point of view. We've got a variety of those points in here, from a variety of sources. Of course, like a game of baseball "Telephone," some of the stories have been told and retold many, many times, with their details blurring and fuzzing as time goes by. It's really a case of hit or myth.

Also, Larsen's game is perhaps the most written-about and most described game in baseball history. There are some incidents that are endlessly reminisced about—homers by Mazeroski, Fisk, Aaron, and others, for instance—but no single game has been as thoroughly discussed and dissected. The game took two hours and nine minutes to play, but has taken almost 50 years to talk about. (A special credit for some of this information goes to Mark Shaw, whose book with Larsen, *The Perfect Yankee*, is the most recent and among the most personal of the many memoirs in which Larsen has participated.)

After joining the Yankees from the St. Louis Browns as part of a massive, 17-player swap, Larsen was 18–3 in 1955 between the Bronx and their Denver farm club, with half of his victories coming in the majors. Heading into the 1956 season, Yankees manager Casey Stengel famously said of Larsen, "That big feller . . . can be a big man in this business—any time he puts his mind to it."

A spring training car accident—at 5:00 A.M., in which a telephone pole and Larsen's vow to settle down took the brunt of the damage—soured the beginning of his 1956 season with the Yankees, and his performance on the hill didn't improve matters. Heading into September, Larsen was 7–5 on a team headed to the World Series, the number four starter on a team that needed only three.

But in September, the man they called "Gooneybird," after some big, awkward cranes seen on the team's offseason trip to Japan, started to develop an odd "no-windup" delivery. He heard that opponents were reading his pitches when he used a full windup and rather than adjust it, he got rid of it. It wasn't really pitching from a set, but was an odd hybrid. He reduced his leg kick to a pump-and-stride, and his glove hand never went above his shoulders. It was quick and it proved to be effective. He won four straight games in September, never allowing more than four hits in any of them. Heading into October, he was on a hot streak.

He cooled off considerably after Stengel gave him the ball to start Game 2 of the World Series against Brooklyn. Staked to a 6–0 lead, Larsen didn't finish two innings, giving up four runs (though unearned) and four walks in a game the Dodgers came back to win 13–8.

"When Casey came out to take the ball away from me, he was mad," Larsen said later. "That made two of us because I was mad, too. I was mad at myself, Casey, the Dodgers, everybody in the world. I was boiling in the clubhouse. I was sure I'd never get another chance to pitch in that Series."

Guess again.

Trailing two games to none, the Yankees rallied to take the next two contests, tying the Series and making Game 5 at Yankee Stadium pivotal. Since both teams were in New York, there were no travel days. After Game 1 was played on October 3, the clubs took Thursday off and then played in Series games for the next six consecutive days.

Among the many issues about Game 5 that create discussion and debate is just exactly what time Larsen got in the night before. There have been several stories printed, each a little different. Author Roger Kahn quoted Yankees outfielder Bob Cerv as saying, "I left him at 4:00 A.M." Sportswriter Arthur Richman, however, may have been toeing a company line when he spoke of leaving Larsen at the pitcher's hotel at midnight, somewhere far short of soused.

> "The million-to-one shot came in. Hell froze over. A month of Sundays hit the calendar. Don Larsen today pitched a no-hit, no-run, no-man-reach-first game in a World Series."
> —Shirley Povich

Larsen delivers a pitch in the fourth inning of his historic performance in Game 5 of the 1956 World Series.

Mickey Mantle has Larsen drinking ginger ale (!) in his book, *My Favorite Summer: 1956*, but even Larsen disputes Mantle's version of events.

Restaurateur Toots Shor famously recalled introducing Larsen to Chief Justice Earl Warren amid his (Shor's, that is, not the former California governor) and Larsen's booze-filled evening.

In his book with Shaw, Larsen, who has also described various versions of the evening, comes clean most recently (. . . and most truthfully? We'll never know . . .).

"One thing is certain," he writes. "I did return to my hotel before midnight."

That might seem like revisionist history to some who believe the other stories, but one fact leads one to believe Larsen: he didn't know that he'd be starting in Game 5 the next day. Believe it or not, Casey Stengel not only had not announced his starter to the press, but he hadn't even told the team or the pitcher. In a game that today sees managers laying out starting rotations weeks in advance sometimes, and with day-before pitching matchups distributed religiously, the baseball world—including Larsen—went to sleep Sunday night, October 7, not knowing who would pitch in the World Series the next afternoon. This uncertainty (though perhaps colored in Larsen's mind by his inept Game 2 performance) makes it unlikely that he would stay out all night because of the off chance he'd be needed the next day. Had he known for sure that he was not going to pitch, it would be easy to see him living the high life. But he didn't know.

In the book he adds, "I would never have gotten myself out of top physical and mental condition on the eve of such an important game."

Again, maybe it's a bit of belated image-polishing, but there are so many conflicting stories about his exploits that the simple story makes the most sense. He went to dinner, went home, and went to sleep.

The way that Larsen finally did find out on Monday morning that he'd take the hill is a very interesting one. Stengel never did speak to him about it. Rather, Larsen found out his role when he arrived in the clubhouse.

"Frankie Crosetti, the third-base coach, placed the pregame warm-up ball in the shoe of the starting pitcher before game time. For me to see that ball there in the shoe probably made my heart stop," Larsen goes on to write.

That's right. The biggest game of Don Larsen's life, and he didn't know he'd be pitching it until two or three hours prior. "Don had a look of disbelief on his face," remembered Hank Bauer. "He saw that ball in the shoe and he took a big gulp."

He had good reason to. The lineup Larsen was facing was the most star-studded lineup that anyone ever beat in a perfect game. It included future Hall of Famers Pee Wee Reese, Duke Snider, Jackie Robinson, and Roy Campanella. The Dodgers' lineup also featured standouts Gil Hodges and Carl Furillo. Brooklyn had won its second straight National League pennant and was hoping to also win two World Series in a row, having defeated the Yankees in the "wait till next year" Series of 1955.

Unlike Game 2, Larsen started out well. He struck out second baseman Jim Gilliam to open the first. He went 3–2 on Reese before getting another strikeout. It was the last three-ball count Larsen reached the rest of the afternoon.

Surprise!

Don Larsen has spent most of the years since that day talking about his perfect game, and he has often said he never gets tired of it. Who would? But he also has written about an interesting fact from the immediate end of the game. While sixty-four thousand fans and thousands more listening or watching on radio or TV knew, and his teammates knew, and the Dodgers knew, the man on the mound says he didn't know. Know what?

"I've said this before, and no one believes me, but I didn't know it was a perfect game until they told me in the clubhouse," he told MSG Network in 2000. "I knew it was a no-hitter, of course, and that we won the game—that was most important. But I didn't know it was perfect."

It was, Don, it was.

In the second inning, Larsen got a little lucky, as perfect-game pitchers are wont to do. Jackie Robinson, leading off, smashed a hard hopper toward third baseman Andy Carey. Carey reached out for the pea, but it glanced off his glove. If the rebound had not gone right to shortstop Gil McDougald, then the speedy Robinson would have made it. As it was, McDougald's throw just nipped Jackie.

With two outs in the bottom of the fourth and Brooklyn's pitcher Sal Maglie one strike from closing out the inning, Mantle came through for Larsen and the 64,519 fans packing Yankee Stadium (the largest crowd ever to see a perfect game). The 1956 Triple Crown winner and eventual American League MVP pulled a Maglie fastball into the right-field seats.

Umpire Babe Pinelli had a great view of Larsen's continuing excellence. "Larsen was a master of control that day," he later told writer Glenn Dickey. "His change of pace was great, curving away from right-handed batters, but the biggest thing was that he was pinpointing his pitches."

The outs kept coming and the anticipation in the stadium kept rising, along with Larsen's nervousness. "After the seventh, I went back in the tunnel to have a cigarette," Larsen said. "And I spoke to Mickey about the game, asked him if he thought I'd get a no-hitter. He just walked away. After that, the dugout was like a morgue."

In the eighth, Robinson grounded out to Larsen on an 0–2 count. Larsen was still throwing strikes, hitting any spot he wanted.

"I never had control like that in my life," he said. Obviously.

While no one in the dugout or on the airwaves was talking about it, everyone in the park knew what was going on, and when Larsen led off the bottom of the eighth, he received a tremendous standing ovation.

And then the ninth . . .

As Carl Furillo stepped to the plate amid the din of Yankee Stadium, Berra spoke to him.

"This guy's got good stuff, huh?" Berra, according to *SI*'s Robert Creamer, said.

Furillo took two pitches, then fouled off three more, then he got a good hold of the sixth pitch, but his long fly ball died short of the wall in right field in Hank Bauer's glove.

Larsen (center, without cap) is hurried off the field after his gem at Yankee Stadium.

One down.

Next up, Roy Campanella. Three-time MVP. One of the best-hitting catchers in baseball until Mike Piazza came along. Four home runs in four previous Series appearances. But the awards didn't matter, as Larsen and catcher Yogi Berra worked their preplanned strategy on Campy perfectly, inducing a weak grounder to second base.

Two outs.

Dodgers manager Walter Alston sent in a pinch-hitter, Dale Mitchell, a little-used but quality outfielder. Mitchell had led the American League in hits in 1949 with Cleveland and would end up a .312 lifetime hitter. He had come over from the Indians in midseason and, like Pinelli, was playing out his string. This Game 5 pinch-hitting appearance in the Series would be his next-to-last big-league at-bat. It would, however, be his most memorable, or should we say, most famous.

"I was so weak in the knees out there, I thought I was going to faint," Larsen recalled. "When Mitchell came up, I was so nervous, I almost fell down. My legs felt rubbery, and my fingers didn't feel like they were on my hand. I said to myself, 'Please help me out, somebody.'"

With every person in the stadium on their feet and every voice exhorting him onward, Larsen fired in ball one to Mitchell, outside.

He threw a slider on the next pitch and it crossed the plate for strike one.

Mitchell swung at Larsen's third pitch, as more than sixty-four thousand fans held their breath. They exhaled when Mitchell missed and the ball plopped into Berra's glove. After a foul ball, pitch number 97 of the day from Larsen headed toward home plate. Larsen writes:

I remember watching the ball turn over and over and head on a direct line with Mitchell's uniform letters. I saw Dale commit himself and make a futile half swing. He didn't connect and then I saw the ball pop squarely into Yogi's mitt.

Instantly, Dale looked back at Pinelli. I watched the umpire's mouth open, and he said something I couldn't understand. A second later, Pinelli's right arm pointed upward toward the sky.

And that was it. Don Larsen had changed history. He had moved the baseball calendar from B.L. to A.L. The noise was thunderous. Yet Larsen's reaction was almost robotic. Instead of collapsing, Cone-like, or exulting like Wells, he simply walked off the mound, as if unsure of what he had done.

In the years since, it has become more and more obvious with every perfect game–less World Series: Larsen had done the impossible.

A Toy Balloon

As one of the most written about sports events of all time, Larsen's perfect game has generated some lovely prose. In his column after the game, Arthur Daley of *The New York Times* summed up the mood of the fans in the stadium in this colorful passage:

Somewhere in the middle of the game the crowd seemed to get a mass realization of the wonders that were being unfolded. Tension kept mounting until it was as brittle as an electric light bulb. The slightest jounce and the dang thing might explode.

Or perhaps it was more like a guy blowing air into a toy balloon. He keeps blowing and blowing with red-faced enthusiasm. But every puff might be the last. Larger and larger grew Larsen's balloon. It was of giant size at the start of the ninth.

DON LARSEN'S PERFECT GAME
OCTOBER 8, 1956

Brooklyn	AB	R	H	RBI
Gilliam, 2b	3	0	0	0
Reese, ss	3	0	0	0
Snider, cf	3	0	0	0
Robinson, 3b	3	0	0	0
Hodges, 1b	3	0	0	0
Amoros, lf	3	0	0	0
Furillo, rf	3	0	0	0
Campanella, c	3	0	0	0
Maglie, p	2	0	0	0
Mitchell, ph	1	0	0	0
Totals	**27**	**0**	**0**	**0**

New York	AB	R	H	RBI
Bauer, rf	4	0	1	1
Collins, 1b	4	0	1	0
Mantle, cf	3	1	1	1
Berra, c	3	0	0	0
Slaughter, lf	2	0	0	0
Martin, 2b	3	0	1	0
McDougald, ss	2	0	0	0
Carey, 3b	3	1	1	0
Larsen, p	2	0	0	0
Totals	**26**	**2**	**5**	**2**

	1	2	3	4	5	6	7	8	9	R	H	E
Br	0	0	0	0	0	0	0	0	0	0	0	0
NYY	0	0	0	1	0	1	0	0	x	2	5	0

Brooklyn	IP	H	R	ER	BB	K
Maglie (L)	8	5	2	2	2	5

New York	IP	H	R	ER	BB	K
Larsen (W)	9	0	0	0	0	7

Time—2:06; Att.—64,519

Catcher Berra jumps into the arms of the only man to pitch a perfect game (or a no-hitter) in the World Series.

Harvey Haddix
12 Perfect Innings
May 26, 1959

Hard-Luck Harvey

For mounting pressure in baseball, nothing is more nerve-racking than a perfect game in progress. On May 26, 1959, Harvey Haddix of the Pittsburgh Pirates retired the first 36 Milwaukee Braves batters in a row. That's right: 36. Twelve innings. A complete game plus three. Some have called it the best game ever pitched . . . almost. But even that wasn't enough for him to pitch a perfect game, for the simple reason that his team couldn't score a run.

Haddix's unprecedented string of consecutive outs is a feat that ranks with the most unassailable in baseball. Yet nowhere in the record book does Haddix receive credit for 12 innings of perfect pitching. In 1991, an eight-man committee on statistical accuracy voted unanimously to define an official perfect game as a game of nine innings or more that ends with no batter reaching first base (in addition, the same pitcher must start and finish the game—see Chapter 8). Since Haddix and the Pirates eventually lost the game, 1–0, in 13 innings, Haddix's otherworldly performance was deleted from the list of perfect games.

"In the long run," a philosophical Haddix said before his death in 1994, "I got more notoriety for losing the game in 13 innings than if I'd have won it in nine."

So the greatest game ever pitched is not a perfect game. But it was still a hell of a game.

During a pregame meeting, Haddix and his catcher, Smoky Burgess, were reviewing the scouting reports and planning their pitching patterns against the powerful Milwaukee batters. The Braves, who were coming off back-to-back World Series appearances, boasted a potent lineup featuring the future Hall of Fame sluggers Henry Aaron and Eddie Mathews. Pittsburgh third baseman Don Hoak, who was eavesdropping on the strategy session, said to Haddix, "Harv, if you pitch like that, you'll throw a no-hitter."

As Haddix warmed up for the game in Milwaukee against Lew Burdette and the Braves, he was not throwing particularly hard, his breaking ball was not especially sharp, and his control was not exactly pinpoint. But once the game started Haddix just got outs. Lots of them. The Braves were swinging early in the count and returned to the bench quickly; Haddix went to three balls on just one batter. When he set the Braves down in order in the seventh, it was apparent that this was more than a no-hitter. Twenty-one Braves had come to bat; all had made outs. No walk or error

had tarnished the game. While Haddix was flawless, Burdette pitched just well enough, holding the Pirates scoreless, too.

Though rain was falling throughout the evening at Milwaukee's County Stadium, foul weather could not dampen Haddix's masterful form. By the end of the eighth inning, he had retired 24 in a row. Three outs to go for a perfect game, but the Pirates still weren't winning, either.

Haddix, bearing down for the ninth inning, struck out two of the three men to face him. The crowd of 19,194 was screaming with every pitch. When Haddix fanned Burdette for the third out in the last of the ninth, he had done something no National League pitcher had accomplished in 79 years—retire the first 27 batters of a game. As Haddix accepted congratulations from teammates, he knew his night's work was far from over.

The scoreless game entered extra innings, and Haddix retired the Braves in order in the tenth. He got them 1-2-3 in the eleventh. And he did it again in the twelfth. But the Pittsburgh batters repeatedly failed to deliver the key hit with runners in scoring position. The Pirates standouts Roberto Clemente and Dick Groat were given the night off by manager Danny Murtaugh, and for reasons Haddix never did understand, neither player got into the game as a pinch-hitter.

"I don't know why Clemente and Groat were out of the lineup," Haddix said. "When you consider we had 12 hits and couldn't score a run, Groat and Clemente might have made the difference."

> "In the long run, I got more notoriety for losing the game in 13 innings than if I'd have won it in nine."
> —Harvey Haddix

Superstitious people view the number 13 as unlucky, and in the bottom of the thirteenth inning, Haddix's fortunes changed. He got two strikes on leadoff batter Felix Mantilla, then threw what he thought was strike three. The umpire disagreed. On the next pitch, Mantilla slapped a routine grounder to the third baseman. Hoak fielded the ball cleanly, but threw a short-hopper in the dirt that first baseman Rocky Nelson was unable to handle. Hoak's throwing error ended the perfect game.

"I'll never forget that play," said Haddix. "Hoak had all night. He picked up the ball, looked at the seams . . . then threw it away."

Haddix's hypnotic pitching spell had ended, but the feat remains legendary today, in an era when pitching a complete game, much less 12 perfect innings, is a rarity.

Ironically, Hoak's pregame prediction held true, for Haddix still had a no-hitter intact. "I wasn't concerned about perfect games and no-hitters. I just wanted to win," said Haddix. With runs tough to come by, the next batter, Mathews, sacrificed Mantilla to second base, and then Aaron was intentionally walked to set up the double play. On deck was Joe Adcock, who

Haddix is noticeably absent from the record books when it comes to perfect games, but his 12 perfect innings in 1959 have never been matched.

Haddix pitched a season in Cincinnati before making history in one of his first starts in a Pirates unfirom.

HARVEY HADDIX'S LOST PERFECT GAME
MAY 26, 1959

Pittsburgh	AB	R	H	RBI
Schofield, ss	6	0	3	0
Virdon, cf	6	0	1	0
Burgess, c	5	0	0	0
Nelson, 1b	5	0	2	0
Skinner, lf	5	0	1	0
Mazeroski, 2b	5	0	1	0
Hoak, 3b	5	0	2	0
Mejias, rf	3	0	1	0
Stuart, ph	1	0	0	0
Christopher, rf	1	0	0	0
Haddix, p	5	0	1	0
Totals	**47**	**0**	**12**	**0**

Milwaukee	AB	R	H	RBI
O'Brien, 2b	3	0	0	0
Rice, ph	1	0	0	0
Mantilla, 2b	1	1	0	0
Mathews, 3b	4	0	0	0
Aaron, rf	4	0	0	0
Adcock, 1b	5	0	1	1
Covington, lf	4	0	0	0
Crandall, c	4	0	0	0
Pafko, cf	4	0	0	0
Logan, ss	4	0	0	0
Burdette, p	4	0	0	0
Totals	**38**	**1**	**1**	**1**

	1	2	3	4	5	6	7	8	9	10	11	12	13	R	H	E
Pitt	0	0	0	0	0	0	0	0	0	0	0	0	0	0	12	1
Mil	0	0	0	0	0	0	0	0	0	0	0	0	1	1	1	0

Pittsburgh	IP	H	R	ER	BB	K
Haddix (L)	12.2	1	1	0	1	8

Milwaukee	IP	H	R	ER	BB	K
Burdette (W)	13	12	0	0	0	2

Time—2:54; Att.—19,194

was 0-for-4 with two strikeouts. Haddix had handled him easily with inside sliders. This time, however, Haddix made the mistake that would haunt him forever. He left a slider too high in the zone, and Adcock smashed the ball over the wall in right-center field for a home run. The no-hitter was gone, the shutout was gone, the victory was gone, all with one swing of the bat.

But a bizarre coda simply added to this game's place in history. As Adcock went into his home-run trot, Mantilla touched the plate as the winning run. Aaron, assuming the game was over, headed across the diamond to celebrate the improbable victory with his teammates. The umpires ruled that Adcock was out for passing Aaron between second base and third. Mantilla's run was the only one that counted, and Adcock's home run was changed to a run-scoring double. The official score of the game is 1–0, but to Haddix, the score is unimportant. "It didn't matter to me whether it was 1–0 or 100–0," he said. "We lost the game, and that's what hurt me most."

Following the game, Burdette joked that he would seek a raise because the greatest pitched game in baseball history wasn't good enough to beat him.

"Obviously, I had no right to win that game," said Burdette. "But that's baseball for you." Indeed, had the Pirates been able to push one runner across home plate in regulation, Haddix would have hurled and won a perfect game. And he would have retired just 27 consecutive batters instead of 36 in a row. What poor Harvey Haddix needed was a run.

Haddix

Going the Distance, Part 2

Forty-three years after Joe Oeschger of the Boston Braves and Leon Cadore of the Brooklyn Robins dueled 26 innings in the longest and most remarkable game ever played, Warren Spahn of the Milwaukee Braves and Juan Marichal of the San Francisco Giants hooked up in a game almost as remarkable.

Although this game ended 10 innings short of the 1920 classic, what made it remarkable was that it came during an era when relief pitchers had burst into prominence; that seven of the participants in the game, including both pitchers, would be elected to the Hall of Fame; and that one of the pitchers was 42 years old.

By the time he took the Candlestick Park mound on the night of July 2, 1963, Spahn had won 20 games or more 12 times in his career and had already won 338 games on his way to 363 wins, a record for a left-hander. At age 42, he would win 23 games, tied for third in the National League; work $259^2/_3$ innings; and pitch seven shutouts, second in the league.

His opponent, Marichal, was a 25-year-old Dominican, known as the "Dominican Dandy," in his fourth major league season. He had won only 49 major league games, but he entered the game with an eight-game winning streak, had pitched a no-hitter against Houston 17 days earlier, and was quickly becoming a force in the National League with his high leg kick and multiple deceptive arm angles. He would win 25 games that season, tied with Sandy Koufax for the league lead, pitch a league high $321^1/_3$ innings, throw five shutouts and 18 complete games, and finish his career with 243 victories).

In addition to the pitchers, future Hall of Famers in the game were Hank Aaron and Eddie Mathews for the Braves, and Willie Mays, Willie McCovey, and Orlando Cepeda for the Giants.

It was obvious from the start that both pitchers were on their games on this cool evening in northern California. Marichal tip-toed around two jams, one in the fourth when Mays threw Norm Larker out at the plate, another in the seventh when a botched hit-and-run play removed Del Crandall from the bases and Spahn followed with a double off the right-field wall.

The Giants got a runner to third in the second inning and put two runners on base in the seventh, but failed to score. The closest they got to a run came in the ninth when McCovey ripped a searing line drive over the right-field fence, just foul by inches. Spahn got through the ninth, and the game went into extra innings, still scoreless.

Giants manager Alvin Dark wanted to take Marichal out of the game after nine, but the young pitcher begged Dark to let him continue.

In the fourteenth inning, the Giants posed their most serious threat off Spahn when Harvey Kuenn led off with a double and Mays drew a walk. But Spahn retired McCovey and Felipe Alou, and after an error loaded the bases, Spahn put down the threat by retiring Ed Bailey. And they went to the fifteenth inning.

Again, Dark wanted to take his young pitcher out of the game. "I told him, 'I'm not leaving while that old guy is still on the mound,'" Marichal said years later. "I kept telling myself, 'OK, just one more inning.' I just didn't want to leave before he did. I didn't want that old man lasting longer than me."

Spahn, who would lead the league with 22 complete games, wasn't going anywhere.

"He was incredible," Marichal said, "and I wound up staying in there a lot longer than I thought I would."

Marichal was just as incredible, actually getting better as the game went on. Through seven innings, he had allowed six hits. When he put the Braves down in the top of the sixteenth, he had held them to two hits and two walks over the last nine innings and, in one stretch, retired 17 consecutive batters.

In the bottom of the sixteenth, Spahn retired the first batter and then faced Willie Mays, who was hitless for the night. Old-timers flashed back to 1951 at the Polo Grounds when a young Mays, just up from the minor leagues, went hitless in his first 12 at-bats in the major leagues. As the story goes, Giants manager Leo Durocher encouraged the 20-year-old rookie by telling him, "You're my center fielder even if you don't get a hit all season."

Mays got his first major league hit, a home run, in his 13th at-bat—off Warren Spahn.

The first pitch to Mays in the bottom of the sixteenth inning at Candlestick Park on the night of July 2, 1963—rather, the early morning of July 3—was a screwball that, according to Spahn, "didn't do anything but float," and Mays drove it into the night, over the left-field fence to give the Giants, and Marichal, a 1–0 victory.

Each pitcher threw more than 200 pitches, and the game took four hours and 10 minutes. When Mays' shot disappeared over the fence, the clock on the Candlestick Park scoreboard read 12:31 A.M.

> " I just didn't want to leave before he did. I didn't want that old man lasting longer than me."
> —Juan Marichal

The Dominican with the signature leg kick, Marichal was in the midst of his breakout season when he outdueled Spahn in one of the more memorable games of the last century.

JUAN MARICHAL/WARREN SPAHN 16-INNING GAME
JULY 2, 1963

Milwaukee	AB	R	H	RBI
Maye, cf	6	0	0	0
Bolling, 2b	7	0	2	0
Aaron, rf	6	0	0	0
Mathews, 3b	2	0	0	0
Menke, 3b	5	0	2	0
Larker, 1b	5	0	0	0
Jones, lf	5	0	1	0
Dillard, lf	1	0	0	0
Crandall, c	6	0	2	0
McMillan, ss	6	0	0	0
Spahn, p	6	0	1	0
Totals	**55**	**0**	**8**	**0**

San Francisco	AB	R	H	RBI
Kuenn, 3b	7	0	1	0
Mays, cf	6	1	1	1
McCovey, lf	6	0	1	0
Alou, rf	6	0	1	0
Cepeda, 1b	6	0	2	0
Bailey, c	6	0	1	0
Pagan, ss	2	0	0	0
Davenport, ph	1	0	0	0
Bowman, ss	3	0	2	0
Hiller, 2b	6	0	0	0
Marichal, p	6	0	0	0
Totals	**55**	**1**	**9**	**1**

	1 2 3	4 5 6	7 8 9	10 11 12	13 14 15	16	R	H	E
Mil	0 0 0	0 0 0	0 0 0	0 0 0	0 0 0	0	0	8	1
SanF	0 0 0	0 0 0	0 0 0	0 0 0	0 0 0	1	1	9	1

Milwaukee	IP	H	R	ER	BB	K
Spahn (L)	15.1	9	1	1	1	2

San Francisco	IP	H	R	ER	BB	K
Marichal (W)	16	8	0	0	4	10

Time—4:10; Att.—15,921

Spahn, who led the league that season with 22 complete games—an unheard-of figure by today's standards—wasn't about to let anyone else finish what he had started.

In a game that featured seven Hall of Famers, Mays (right, receiving thanks from Marichal) threw
a runner out at the plate and homered for the game's only run.

A Father's Day to Remember

Eighty-four years of National League history passed between the first perfect game pitched in the "senior circuit" and the second. The first was John M. Ward, a hard-throwing future lawyer, way back in the day. The second was by a hard-throwing future United States senator on Father's Day, 1964. It's fitting that Jim Bunning performed this once-in-fourscore feat on that day, as nine kids (eight at the time) called him Dad. With a house that crowded, he probably enjoyed the solitude of the pitcher's mound.

It was a hot, steamy, muggy day in Queens when Bunning took the hill against the lowly Mets. This was his first season in Philly after nine years in the American League, highlighted by his 1958 no-hitter for Detroit and his 1959 and 1960 AL strikeout championships. Against leadoff hitter Jim Hickman, Bunning remembered, "I got away with a couple there." But Hickman went down, the first of 27 straight.

"As the game went on, all the pitches were working well," Bunning recalled from his senate office. "The slider, curve, and fastball all got thrown to the areas I was trying to throw them to. I was ahead of all the hitters, which also made it much easier."

It was 2–0 Philly by the fifth when Mets catcher Jesse Gonder nearly clipped Bunning's string of zeroes. "I threw him the only change-up I threw all game, and he almost got a base hit," Bunning said. But a nice play up the middle by second baseman Tony Taylor caught the slow-footed Gonder.

In the sixth, Bunning himself rapped a double off the wall to drive in two more runs. By then it was obvious that he was working on something special. But his reaction to this possibility was something not so special, but rather extraordinary. He talked about it.

Any baseball fan worth his salted peanuts knows that you never talk

> "The slider, curve, and fastball all got thrown to the areas I was trying to throw them to. I was ahead of all the hitters, which also made it much easier."
> —Jim Bunning

Bonus Baby

"The perfect game continued to follow me in that people kept reminding me of it," Bunning said of his 1964 gem. He got another reminder on June 21, 1997, the 33rd anniversary of his Father's Day perfect game, when the Bunnings welcomed a new grandson, James Lewis Bunning. Another perfect day for Granddad.

about a no-hitter (or a perfect game) while it's going on. You'll find several stories in this book about pitchers avoiding any discussion they might have overheard. But Bunning was the one *starting* the conversations in his game.

"He was jabbering like a magpie," said catcher Gus Triandos.

"He was coming back to the dugout yelling at the guys and counting down the outs," recalled manager Gene Mauch.

"I didn't care about superstitions," Bunning said. "It was important to me to relax. Having gone through one no-hitter [in Fenway Park for the Tigers] really helped me in the perfect game. No one said anything then, and when it was over, it was total bedlam. I didn't want that to happen again, so I tried to talk about it at Shea."

By the ninth, Bunning's jersey was dripping wet. After getting the first two outs quickly, he needed a moment, and called Triandos out to the mound. "He wanted me to tell him a joke," said Triandos. "But I couldn't think of anything."

No jokes and five pitches later, all curveballs, pinch-hitter John Stephenson was out number 27. Bunning had pitched the first perfecto in the NL since 1880 and the first in baseball's regular season since 1922.

While some perfect-game pitchers enjoyed big postgame celebrations, trips to the morning talk shows, and salutes from near and far, part of Bunning's reward was far more prosaic. He made an appearance on the *Ed Sullivan Show* and did numerous interviews. Bunning says that he wanted to carry the celebration to legendary New York nightspot Toots Shor's, but it was closed.

Bunning and his wife ended up at a Howard Johnson's on the Jersey Turnpike. *Sic transit gloria*, just about as fast as the Mets had transited from home plate back to the dugout.

Bunning already owned one no-hitter, earned as a member of the AL's Detroit Tigers.

JIM BUNNING'S PERFECT GAME
JUNE 21, 1964

Philadelphia	AB	R	H	RBI
Briggs, cf	4	1	0	0
Herrnstein, 1b	4	0	0	0
Callison, rf	4	1	2	1
Allen, 3b	3	0	1	1
Covington, lf	2	0	0	0
Wine, pr/ss	1	1	0	0
Taylor, 2b	3	2	1	0
Rojas, ss/lf	3	0	1	0
Triandos, c	4	1	2	2
Bunning, p	4	0	1	2
Totals	**32**	**6**	**8**	**6**

New York	AB	R	H	RBI
Hickman, cf	3	0	0	0
Hunt, 2b	3	0	0	0
Kranepool, 1b	3	0	0	0
Christopher, rf	3	0	0	0
Gonder, c	3	0	0	0
Taylor, lf	3	0	0	0
Smith, ss	3	0	0	0
Samuel, 3b	2	0	0	0
Altman, ph	1	0	0	0
Stallard, p	1	0	0	0
Wakefield, p	1	0	0	0
Kanehl, ph	1	0	0	0
Sturdivant, p	0	0	0	0
Stevenson, ph	1	0	0	0
Totals	**27**	**0**	**0**	**0**

	1	2	3	4	5	6	7	8	9	R	H	E
Phil	1	1	0	0	0	4	0	0	0	6	8	0
NYY	0	0	0	0	0	0	0	0	0	0	0	0

Philadelphia	IP	H	R	ER	BB	K
Bunning (W)	9	0	0	0	0	10

New York	IP	H	R	ER	BB	K
Stallard (L)	5.2	7	6	6	4	3
Wakefield	0.1	0	0	0	0	0
Sturdivant	3	1	0	0	0	3

Time—2:19; Att.—32,026

CHAPTER 20

CHAPTER 20

Bunning's fall-away form was relatively new to National League hitters after he'd spent nine years baffling American League lineups.

The scoreboard says it all at Shea Stadium in New York, where Bunning set the Mets down in his Father's Day no-hitter.

Perfect as Perfect Gets

If there is one pitcher in this pantheon of unhittables who might be called the "most unhittable," a stadium full of baseball experts might pick this unassuming yet ultracompetitive lefty from Brooklyn.

Few, if any, pitchers enjoy the immensely positive reputation that Sandy Koufax earned with a stunning string of five seasons in the early 1960s during which he won five ERA titles, three Cy Young Awards, an MVP trophy, set a single-season strikeout record, threw a no-hitter each year from 1962 to 1965—the last being a perfect game—and helped the Dodgers win three NL pennants and two World Series championships. No pitcher has ever had as remarkable, as memorable, or as dominating a five-season run.

"There were days that Koufax would pace the dugout before games and just tell his teammates, 'Give me one run, that's all I need,'" says Ed Gruver, author of the 1999 biography *Koufax*. "That's the kind of confidence he had that he could shut the other team down when he had his really good stuff."

And playing for the Dodgers in those days, one run was often all he got. Los Angeles lived and died with speed, defense, and pitching.

"That was the year [1965] we hit .245 [seventh in the NL] as a team and won the championship," recalled Jeff Torborg, then a second-year catcher. "Our leading hitter was [pitcher Don] Drysdale, who was often our right-handed pinch-hitter. In fact, in 1964, when Sandy pitched his third no-hitter, Drysdale was not at the park. When someone called him that night to tell him that Sandy had pitched a no-hitter, Drysdale asked, 'Did he win?' That gives you an indication of how much confidence we had in our offense."

Along with worrying about his offense, Koufax worried about his left arm—his elbow, to be precise. The same wondrous appendage that carried him to stardom would be the anchor that would eventually drag him down and out of baseball. By 1965, arthritis was causing Koufax daily pain. There had been talk of him missing more of the season, but he soldiered on with little medical help. Koufax took drugs to reduce inflammation. The pitcher smeared on Capsolin, an ointment that helped him loosen up his muscles. Postgame, he dunked the elbow for up to 30 minutes in an ice bath wearing a protective rubber sleeve devised by the Dodgers trainers.

Koufax kept going out there, however, with an intensity that belied his quiet demeanor. Few pitchers in history had Koufax's skills, fewer still had his drive to win. He was satisfied with nothing less than victory.

> "He did have his live fastball, but he didn't have his real good stuff early. Of course, that was great stuff for everyone else, but not for him."
> —Dodgers catcher Jeff Torborg

Fans around the National League responded to his talent and his grit, turning out in droves every night he pitched. *The New York Times*' Leonard Koppett did a little figuring and noted that Koufax's appearances in 1965 averaged more than thirty-six thousand fans; the NL average for all games was just over fifteen thousand. "His 'personal attendance,' in his 40 starts," wrote Koppett, "[will] exceed the total of the Yankees and a majority of the other teams for their 81-game home schedules."

More than twenty-nine thousand of those fans were in attendance on a slightly damp, coolish evening in Chavez Ravine for an odd one-game "series" with the Cubs on September 9. ("It was hardly worth the trip," Koufax wrote in his 1967 autobiography.) The Dodgers trailed the first-place San Francisco Giants by a game; the Giants had put together a 15-game winning streak to catch and pass L.A., so the Dodgers were eager to climb back into first place.

Torborg, who caught for Koufax that night, remembered nothing remarkable about Koufax or the team before this game, though he did delight in pointing out that in those days, the starters warmed up off of a mound located in front of the dugouts, "so that fans can see the pitchers getting ready up close."

As the L.A. crowd filtered in, Cubs center fielder Don Young stepped to the plate to lead off. Koufax wound up and delivered the first pitch of what would become an historic night . . . and bounced a curveball three feet in front of home plate. Not exactly an auspicious beginning, but he wound up getting Young to pop to second base.

The second batter, second baseman Glenn Beckert, then hit a liner that was "about this much foul," remembered Torborg, holding his fingers an inch apart. Beckert then struck out, as did Billy Williams, beginning Koufax's game-long string of at least one strikeout per frame.

"Sandy didn't have a real good curveball early in the game, kind of rolling," Torborg said. "He did have his live fastball, but he didn't have his real good stuff early. Of course, that was great stuff for everyone else, but not for him."

In the second, future Hall of Famer Ernie Banks was Koufax's next strikeout victim, going down swinging for the second out. Left fielder Byron Browne then hit a hard liner to center that Willie Davis caught about waist high, the only fair ball that truly was hit hard against Koufax all night.

Things were going pretty much as planned—at least according to Sandy's plan, that is.

Koufax had stymied Chicago before, fanning 14 Cubs during this two-hitter at Wrigley Field in 1961.

"I didn't talk to Sandy during that game, but that wasn't unusual," said Torborg. "I stayed away from him. I was in awe of him anyway. . . . Later on, though, I sure wasn't going to be the one who said anything [about the perfect game].

"He knew what he wanted to do. I just asked him what he wanted to do before the game. Nowadays, we have meetings with the whole staff. Used to be that before the first game of a series, we'd meet just in general. We didn't go over how we'd pitch every guy. Sandy let me know how he wanted to pitch them."

And when the 800-pound gorilla talks to a second-year catcher, the kid listens.

In the third inning, Koufax finally, tentatively, tried a few fastballs as his arm slowly loosened up.

"It took him a while," Torborg remembered. "He stuck with almost all curveballs for . . . the first three innings. He started to get the fastball over then and that was his strikeout pitch."

Koufax struck out opposing pitcher Bob Hendley to end the third and was through the order perfectly for the first time. Unfortunately, the same was true for the banjo-hitting Trolley Dodgers. In fact, while Koufax kept the Cubs from the bases through five innings, Hendley also didn't allow a base runner until left fielder Lou Johnson opened the bottom of the fifth with a walk.

That season, the Dodgers manufactured so many runs they should have painted their batting helmets yellow. The only run they would provide for Koufax on this night was a typical "Dodger home run."

With Johnson at first, Ron Fairly laid down a perfect sacrifice bunt and Johnson was on second with one out. Early in Jim Lefebvre's at-bat, Johnson broke for third, but Cubs catcher Chris Krug threw the ball into left field, and Johnson scored an easy unearned run. (If you're scoring at home, that's yet another perfect game saved by an opponent's miscue: see Richmond, Joss, Witt, and Browning.)

Ironically, it was a throw that Krug probably shouldn't have made. "I had third stolen easy," Johnson said afterward. "Krug told me that the next time I came up to bat."

Now Hendley, who retired Lefebvre and Wes Parker to end the fifth, was pitching a no-hitter . . . and losing to a perfect game.

Koufax commented after the game on the effect of the close score. "Naturally a pitcher would rather have four or five runs, especially in the last couple of innings. Early on, a tight score might help you pitch better. You have to bear down on every pitch. With an eight- or nine-run lead, it would have been a very different game."

By the sixth inning, players and fans were well aware of the unique pitching duel they were either taking part in or witnessing. Torborg claimed some level of ignorance while also admitting to the pressure he was facing.

"I didn't think about the crowd at all," he said. "I was so involved in the game. They might have been cheering every pitch, I don't remember that at all.

"You could be hearing your own heartbeat. You want to do everything right. Your heart's pounding. You look up to see a no-hitter, but I don't remember when I thought of a perfect game."

"Around the seventh inning we knew Sandy wasn't going to give us a hit," said Hendley. "He was just unbelievably fast."

SANDY KOUFAX'S PERFECT GAME
SEPTEMBER 9, 1965

Chicago	AB	R	H	RBI
Young, cf	3	0	0	0
Beckert, 2b	3	0	0	0
Williams, rf	3	0	0	0
Santo, 3b	3	0	0	0
Banks, 1b	3	0	0	0
Browne, lf	3	0	0	0
Krug, c	3	0	0	0
Kessinger, ss	2	0	0	0
Amalfitano, ph	1	0	0	0
Hendley, p	2	0	0	0
Kuenn, ph	1	0	0	0
Totals	**27**	**0**	**0**	**0**

Dodgers	AB	R	H	RBI
Wills, ss	3	0	0	0
Gilliam, 3b	3	0	0	0
Kennedy, 3b	0	0	0	0
Davis, cf	3	0	0	0
Johnson, lf	2	1	1	0
Fairly, rf	2	0	0	0
Lefebvre, 2b	3	0	0	0
Tracewski, 2b	0	0	0	0
Parker, 1b	3	0	0	0
Torborg, c	3	0	0	0
Koufax, p	2	0	0	0
Totals	**24**	**1**	**1**	**0**

	1	2	3	4	5	6	7	8	9	R	H	E
Chi	0	0	0	0	0	0	0	0	0	0	0	1
LA	0	0	0	0	1	0	0	0	x	1	1	0

Chicago	IP	H	R	ER	BB	K
Hendley (L)	8	1	1	0	1	3

Los Angeles	IP	H	R	ER	BB	K
Koufax (W)	9	0	0	0	0	14

Time—1:43; Att.—29,139

"Around the seventh I thought a no-hitter was in reach," said Koufax. "And believe me, I really wanted it. I didn't think too much about the perfect game. No one said a word to me about what was going on, but I knew and so did everyone else."

With two outs in the seventh Koufax reached the only 3–0 count of the evening, to Billy Williams, the only lefty in the Cubs' lineup. But then he grooved two strikes past a frozen Williams, who hit the sixth pitch to Johnson in left for the third out.

In the bottom of that inning, Hendley finally cracked, but just barely. He had been matching Koufax zero for zero, with only the walk to Johnson marring his record. Johnson came up again with two outs in the bottom of the seventh and lifted a soft fly ball behind first base. Former MVP shortstop Ernie Banks was playing first and he gave chase. The ball flopped to the ground just beyond his outstretched mitt, and the speedy Johnson made it to second. Johnson was actually the only player to reach base in the game for either team.

With a one-run lead and the stuff he was showing to the Cubs, for the rest of the game a catcher was really all Koufax would need. The other Dodgers

Koufax (No. 32) is congratulated by teammates after his 1965 perfect game in Los Angeles.

were just as much spectators as the fans in the stands during the eighth and ninth innings as Koufax put on a masterful display of strikeout pitching.

"In the eighth, Ron Santo led off and went up 2–0 before Sandy hooked him three straight times," Torborg remembered. "Santo walked back to the dugout, and he knew: 'It's over, boys. Oh, boy, here we go,' he seemed to say."

"I've never seen Sandy throw as hard as he did when he struck me out in the eighth," Santo said. "He threw one fastball right by and I was waiting for it. He seemed to get a burst of energy in the last innings."

Banks went down swinging, thus making his night a perfect three-for-three—strikeouts, that is.

Browne also went down swinging. Koufax seemed to grow stronger and stronger as the night went on. Meanwhile, Hendley continued to shut down the Dodgers, save for one unearned run. A harder-luck pitching story has never been written. A player so anonymous that he could have had "journey-man" written on the back of his uniform had come into Dodger Stadium, held the eventual world champs to a walk, a hit, and a measly unearned run, and he would leave that night with nothing but a tired arm for his trouble.

And so, on to the ninth.

"Krug threw a ball away to let in our only run, and he led off the ninth inning," noted Torborg. "I remember thinking, if anyone wants to redeem himself, it's Krug."

Up in the press box Vin Scully continued his remarkable call of the game to the Dodger radio audience. Scully had been on Armed Forces Radio for Don Larsen's game and would go on to call both Tom Browning's and Dennis Martinez's . . . an amazing four perfect performances at the mike.

At 0–2 to Krug, Scully said, "You can almost taste the pressure now. Koufax lifts his cap, runs his fingers through his black hair, then pulls the cap back down low, fussing at the bill."

The drama continued as Krug took a ball outside, fouled off two pitches, then took ball two. "There are twenty-nine thousand people here tonight," said Scully, "and a million butterflies."

Krug swung and missed at yet another fastball and Koufax was two outs away.

Pinch hitting for shortstop Don Kessinger was Joe Amalfitano, a light-hitting utility player.

"I only called one curveball in the last three innings," said Torborg. "That was to the second hitter, Amalfitano. He'd already gotten big pinch-hits off fastballs on us earlier in the season. So I didn't want to give him a fastball. We called a curve on the second pitch and he fouled it off."

After that foul ball, Scully noted that Koufax took a walk behind the mound, and the Hall of Fame announcer said, "I would think that the mound at Dodger Stadium is the loneliest place in the world."

Koufax came back from his lonely place with another stunning fastball and Amalfitano was out hacking.

On the way back to the dugout, Amalfitano reportedly looked at pinch-hitter Harvey Kuenn and said, "Harvey, you might as well not even bother coming to the plate."

Kuenn bothered anyway. He was batting for the hard-luck Hendley. Kuenn, a former batting champion, must have been experiencing an unpleas-ant sense of déjà vu. Two years earlier, then with the Giants, he had bounced out to end Koufax's second no-hitter.

Kuenn took the first fastball for a strike and watched the next two go by high and tight for balls; on the first of those, Koufax threw so hard that he lost his hat on the follow-through. Scully noted that the hat went so far that Torborg actually got up and retrieved it.

A mighty swing by Kuenn on a high, hard one hit nothing but air, and the count moved to 2–2. The Dodger Stadium crowd, already screaming at top voice, reached a crescendo as Koufax went into his familiar kick with the right leg before flinging his arm and body plateward. With velocity that barely wavered from earlier innings, Koufax zinged a fastball that Kuenn barely saw, let alone hit, and it was over.

Opening Acts

Sandy Koufax was the first pitcher with four no-hitters. He threw one in each season from 1962 to 1965, capped off by his 1965 perfect game. Here are some details of his first three no-hitters, sort of the single, double, and triple of the pitching cycle he completed with his 1965 "homer."

June 30, 1962
Dodgers 5, Mets 0
At Los Angeles

It was Koufax's first no-hitter in the majors, and talk about your good beginnings—he struck out the first three Mets on nine pitches, the first time that feat had been accomplished since 1924. In her spectacularly written masterpiece, *Sandy Koufax: A Lefty's Legacy*, Jane Leavy quoted Mets manager Casey Stengel as saying, "You put the whammy on him when he's pitchin', but when he's pitchin' the whammy tends to go on vacation."

May 11, 1963
Dodgers 8, Giants 0
At San Francisco

Koufax had a perfect game going until the bottom of the eighth. He walked Ed Bailey to break it up, but escaped without another base runner. Tommy Davis in left field had made a nice running catch on a deep drive by Felipe Alou, but the Giants had rarely challenged Koufax. Harvey Kuenn, for what would be the first of two times in his career, made the last out of the no-hitter, this time on a tapper back to Koufax.

June 4, 1964
Dodgers 3, Phillies 0
At Philadelphia

Leavy tells a remarkable story in her 2002 biography of Koufax. Before this start against Philadelphia, Koufax had been struggling a bit. In the locker room, he happened to see a magazine photo that showed, to his trained eye, a small flaw in his delivery. This was not a good omen for the Phillies. Koufax allowed only one walk, in the fourth to Richie Allen. Leavy reports that Phillies manager Gene Mauch tried to break up the pitcher's rhythm with a series of slow-walking pinch-hitters called in from the bullpen, but to no avail. Koufax polished off the Phillies as easily as he downed a postgame beer in celebration.

Koufax had done it, not only pitching a perfect game, but becoming the first pitcher ever with four no-hitters (and in consecutive seasons, no less.). He had struck out the last six hitters he faced, and seven of the last nine. His 14 strikeouts were the most ever in a perfect game.

Koufax was surrounded by teammates, a big grin plastered on his face. They corralled him into the dugout as he waved to the crowd. No one

CHAPTER 21

Nothing but goose eggs on the board when Koufax tossed his perfect game against the awestruck Cubs.

In the Cubs' locker room, the veterans could only shake their heads in wonder. "That man could drive you to drink," said a grumbling Ron Santo.

Banks asked a couple of younger players, "Are you sure you want to play in the National League?"

Back-up catcher Ed Bailey, who had just witnessed his fifth no-hitter as a player, was the calmest of the bunch. "He didn't bother me any." Of course, Bailey didn't play.

"I've seen all the no-hitters he's pitched," Dodgers manager Walter Alston said, "And I'd have to say that he had his greatest stuff in this one."

Koufax was exuberant afterward, but in the somewhat subdued way that he had. He was no David Wells, after all, but a somewhat shy and reserved man who kept his focus where it mattered: on the field. Dodgers owner Walter O'Malley sent champagne to the locker room, but Koufax had a beer instead.

Koufax also toasted his team-mates. "As much as I wanted that no-hitter and the perfect game," Koufax told reporters. "I was just as pleased that I won my 22nd game. I had five starts at it before getting that win and the guys were beginning to think there was something wrong with me."

thought of arthritis or inflammation or pain, they just reveled in the stunning beauty and awesome power of his performance, and indeed in the remarkable rarity of the event they had just witnessed.

A "cleaner" game has never been played in the history of the major leagues. There has never been a complete-game double no-hitter, and so this game set a record that can only be beaten by one: fewest hits, both teams, one game. Johnson was the only player to safely reach base, on a walk and his double. The Cubs' 27 plate appearances joined the Dodgers' 26 to exceed the minimum for the game (with the home team coming up only eight times) by only two, a stunning accomplishment for the pitchers and defenses, and a stirring display of ineptitude by the hitters. Talk about a pitcher's duel . . . this was perhaps the ultimate such duel, as proven by the record.

Of course, as history has shown, there was something wrong with him. Chronic arthritis was wreaking havoc with the tender tendons of his left elbow. To the dismay of the Dodgers fans and the joy of National League batters, by the end of 1966, a little over a year later, Sandy Koufax was gone, retired from the game at the age of 31.

What he left behind, in this game and in his brilliant career, was perhaps baseball's most developed sense of mastery, of the prime example of perfect skill matched with perfect mental makeup. Thousands of pitchers have had great stuff, thousands more wonderful pitching minds. In Koufax, more than in any other player, the wonderful alchemy of athletic achieve-ment reached its highest state of perfection.

Catfish Reels One In

In 1968 he was a two-time All-Star without a winning record to his name. He was three years removed from his high school team in North Carolina. And he did not yet sport the mustache that would grace his Hall of Fame plaque. In fact, he had only been called "Catfish" for a couple of years. Maverick A's owner Charlie Finley felt that "Jim Hunter" wasn't catchy enough. Hearing that the former farm boy had done some fishing back home, Finley dubbed his bonus baby "Catfish Hunter." Fiction or fact, it stuck, and the kid was on his way.

But before he could earn all those World Series rings with Oakland and the Yankees, before he would reel off five straight 20-win seasons, he was on a young and struggling A's team playing in a brand-new ballpark they called the "Oakland Mausoleum."

"It was a very forbidding ballpark," remembered sportswriter Ron Fimrite, later a *Sports Illustrated* regular, but then a local beat writer. "It certainly earned its nickname. It was ugly and spare, not a good place for baseball."

But Hunter had found his home. "I loved pitching there," he wrote in his autobiography. "The foul areas were the biggest in baseball . . . plus the ball never carried at night."

The game on May 8 started not at night, but at dusk, at the unusual hour of 6:00 P.M. Hunter faced the Minnesota Twins, three years removed from a World Series appearance, but still boasting two future Hall of Famers (Harmon Killebrew and Rod Carew) and a perennial batting champ (Tony Oliva).

The game moved rapidly and relatively incident free for the first five or six innings. A few fans and some writers were sitting up and taking notice of all the zeroes, but like all ballplayers, Hunter was having none of it. As he got a drink between innings, he heard a reserve outfielder ask someone else, "Didn't someone get on in the early innings?"

"I didn't want to hear any of that conversation," Hunter wrote, taking part in the long-lived baseball superstition about not talking about an in-progress no-hitter.

A key at-bat came in the seventh against Killebrew, already twice a strikeout victim. Hunter went to 3–2, flirting with imperfection. Then he came in with an off-speed pitch that had Killer so far out in front that he not only missed the ball, but the bat slipped out of his hand and helicoptered toward Hunter's head. He ducked, and the inning was over.

"The greatest and gutsiest pitch of the game," A's manager Bob Kennedy said afterward.

The A's finally scored in the seventh to help their man, after needing to make only a handful of defensive gems to keep perfection alive. One came in the third, a shoestring catch by Joe Rudi in left of a low liner.

Hunter was great at the plate, too, lacing a double in the third, laying down an RBI bunt in the seventh, and hitting a two-run single in the eighth. Ironically, Kennedy had kicked Hunter out of the batting cage before the game, trying to keep to his hitters' schedule. After the game, Hunter, referring to that incident, asked Kennedy, "Can I hit now?" Kennedy said, "Kid, you can do anything you want!"

Center fielder Rick Monday recalled that as the ninth inning progressed, "You could even feel people breathe in unison. With each pitch and call, there was a full exhale. You could feel it get more and more labored as the game and the final inning went on."

After two quick outs, pinch-hitter Rich Reese made Hunter work for history. The pinch-hitter fouled off four straight 3–2 pitches before finally swinging and missing one to end it.

That end was actually a beginning in many ways, however. By 1970, Hunter was the winning ace on a winning team, and in 1971 he started his 20-win streak. Then came the A's three-peat of World Series wins, with Hunter going 4–0 in those title runs.

He moved on to the Yankees as the first big-money free agent (signing a five-year, $3.75 million deal after the 1974 season) and three more Series appearances.

Sadly, Hunter is the only perfect-game pitcher since Charley Robertson who is not still around to enjoy his fame. Hunter contracted Lou Gehrig's disease in 1998. He died in 1999 as the result of injuries from a fall at his home.

Among the many memories he left, including that magical night in 1968, were the dignity, grace, and courage with which he faced his final days that created a more lasting impression.

> Hunter was great at the plate, too, lacing a double in the third, laying down an RBI bunt in the seventh, and hitting a two-run single in the eighth.

Hunter, clean-shaven and barely known as "Catfish" then, was in the early stages of his Hall-of-Fame career when he set down the Twins in order in 1968.

CATFISH HUNTER'S PERFECT GAME
MAY 8, 1968

Minnesota	AB	R	H	RBI
Tovar, 3b	3	0	0	0
Carew, 2b	3	0	0	0
Killebrew, 1b	3	0	0	0
Oliva, rf	3	0	0	0
Uhlaender, cf	3	0	0	0
Allison, lf	3	0	0	0
Hernandez, ss	2	0	0	0
Roseboro, ph	1	0	0	0
Look, c	3	0	0	0
Boswell, p	2	0	0	0
Perranoski, p	0	0	0	0
Reese, ph	1	0	0	0
Totals	**27**	**0**	**0**	**0**

Oakland	AB	R	H	RBI
Campaneris, ss	4	0	2	0
Jackson, rf	4	0	0	0
Bando, 3b	3	0	1	0
Webster, 1b	4	1	2	0
Donaldson, 2b	3	0	0	0
Pagliaroni, c	3	1	0	0
Monday, cf	3	2	2	0
Rudi, lf	3	0	0	0
Robinson, ph	0	0	0	0
Cater, ph	0	0	0	1
Hershberger, lf	0	0	0	0
Hunter, p	4	0	3	3
Totals	**31**	**4**	**10**	**4**

	1	2	3	4	5	6	7	8	9	R	H	E
Minn	0	0	0	0	0	0	0	0	0	0	0	1
Oak	0	0	0	0	0	0	1	3	x	4	10	0

Minnesota	IP	H	R	ER	BB	K
Boswell (L)	7.2	9	4	4	5	6
Perranoski	0.1	1	0	0	0	0

Oakland	IP	H	R	ER	BB	K
Hunter (W)	9	0	0	0	0	11

Time—2:28; Att.—6,298

Oakland A's teammates Jim Pagliaroni (No. 17) and Sal Bando congratulate Hunter after his perfect performance.

Gaylord's Greatest Day

In 17 major league seasons, all with the St. Louis Cardinals, Hall of Famer Bob Gibson won 251 games, pitched a no-hitter, hurled 56 shutouts, pitched seven straight complete-game World Series victories (two of them seventh games and two of them shutouts), and set a World Series single game record in 1968 when he struck out 17 Detroit Tigers. Yet when he was asked to name the best game he ever pitched, Gibson chose one that he lost.

It came against the Giants in San Francisco late in the 1968 season, the season in which Gibson set a major league record with a phenomenal 1.12 earned run average. On September 17, in front of a sparse crowd of 9,546 at Candlestick Park, Gibson was matched up with another future Hall of Famer, Gaylord Perry.

"I lost the game, 1–0," Gibson recalled. "I pitched a four-hitter and Perry pitched a no-hitter. He was so good that day, I felt we couldn't do a thing against him."

The only run came on Gibson's first pitch to the Giants' first batter of the game, Ron Hunt.

> "I thought, 'This guy can't hit the ball out,' so I laid the first pitch right in there . . . and he hit it out. And that was the game."
> —Bob Gibson

"I thought, 'This guy can't hit the ball out' [Hunt hit only 39 home runs in 12 major league seasons, only two that year, and started the day batting .245], so I laid the first pitch right in there . . . and he hit it out. And that was the game."

Gibson, who began the game with a 21–7 record and a 1.13 ERA, gave up hits to Bobby Bonds, Barry's father, Hal Lanier, and Ty Cline, but never was in serious trouble after Hunt's home run.

Perry was even better. The only threats to his no-hitter came in the sixth inning when the pitcher himself stabbed a smash back to the mound hit by Dal Maxvill, and when first baseman Willie McCovey stretched his full 6'4" to snare a scorcher in the hole between first and second off the bat of Bobby Tolan and flipped to Perry covering first for the out.

Gibson struck out 10 Giants. Perry, who entered the game with a record of 14–14, struck out nine and allowed just two balls to be hit to the outfield. Each pitcher walked two. The game was played in an hour and 40 minutes.

"One thing that stands out about that game," said Gibson, "is that the big guy behind home plate [umpire Harry Wendelstedt] didn't miss a call all day."

It may be surprising that Gibson chose this game as his best. Not only was it a defeat, it came at the end of the season with the Cardinals safely in front in the National League pennant race. His World Series record 17 strikeouts against the Tigers in Game 1 of the 1968 World Series, his 13 strikeouts against the Yankees in Game 5 of the 1964 World Series, and his five-hit shutout of the Red Sox in Game 4 of the 1967 World Series received much more attention.

"You strike out a lot of guys in the World Series because the hitters don't know you," Gibson explained. "Not to make light of a World Series game, but they mean more to fans and the media than they do to the players. I tried to go into a game against the [last place] Mets in April with only a few thousand fans in the stands with the same focus and mentality as I did in a game against the Yankees in the World Series."

As a postscript to Gibson's duel with Gaylord Perry on September 17, 1968, on the next day, Ray Washburn of the Cardinals pitched a no-hitter and beat the Giants, 2–0, the first time in major league history that no-hitters were pitched in the same ballpark on consecutive days.

Despite his own no-hitter among 251 career wins, when asked about his "best game," Gibson chose an opposing pitcher's day in the sun.

Perry's no-hitter for San Francisco was matched the following day by St. Louis' Ray Washburn (right) to create some Candlestick Park history.

GAYLORD PERRY'S NO-HITTER
SEPTEMBER 17, 1968

St. Louis	AB	R	H	RBI
Tolan, lf	4	0	0	0
Flood, cf	4	0	0	0
Maris, rf	3	0	0	0
Cepeda, 1b	3	0	0	0
McCarver, c	3	0	0	0
Shannon, 3b	2	0	0	0
Gagliano, 2b	2	0	0	0
Maxvill, ss	2	0	0	0
Edwards, ph	1	0	0	0
Schofield, ss	0	0	0	0
Gibson, p	2	0	0	0
Brock, ph	1	0	0	0
Totals	**27**	**0**	**0**	**0**

San Francisco	AB	R	H	RBI
Bonds, cf	3	0	1	0
Hunt, 2b	3	1	1	1
Cline, lf	3	0	1	0
McCovey, 1b	3	0	0	0
Hart, 3b	3	0	0	0
Davenport, 3b	0	0	0	0
Marshall, rf	2	0	0	0
Mays, cf	1	0	0	0
Dietz, c	2	0	0	0
Lanier, ss	3	0	1	0
Perry, p	3	0	0	0
Totals	**26**	**1**	**4**	**1**

	1	2	3	4	5	6	7	8	9		R	H	E
StL	0	0	0	0	0	0	0	0	0		0	0	0
SanF	1	0	0	0	0	0	0	0	0		1	4	0

St. Louis	IP	H	R	ER	BB	K
Gibson (L)	8	4	1	1	2	10

San Francisco	IP	H	R	ER	BB	K
Perry (W)	9	0	0	0	2	9

Time—1:44; Att.—9,546

CHAPTER 23

PART III

Yesterday
1969 to 1994

Buzzie Bavasi's Top 20 Pitchers of All Time

1. Sandy Koufax
2. Bob Gibson
3. Warren Spahn
4. Bob Feller
5. Carl Hubbell
6. Nolan Ryan
7. Roger Clemens
8. Don Newcombe
9. Tom Seaver
10. Randy Johnson
11. Juan Marichal
12. Lefty Grove
13. Steve Carlton
14. Early Wynn
15. Ferguson Jenkins
16. Dazzy Vance
17. Jim Palmer
18. Don Drysdale
19. Robin Roberts
20. Dizzy Dean

Joe Garagiola's Top 20 Pitchers of All Time

1. Walter Johnson
2. Sandy Koufax
3. Bob Feller
4. Warren Spahn
5. Grover Cleveland Alexander
6. Lefty Grove
7. Cy Young
8. Christy Mathewson
9. Whitey Ford
10. Randy Johnson
11. Bob Gibson
12. Tom Seaver
13. Steve Carlton
14. Carl Hubbell
15. Robin Roberts
16. Juan Marichal
17. Ferguson Jenkins
18. Jim Palmer
19. Nolan Ryan
20. Roger Clemens

Seasons in the Sun

What is the greatest single-season pitching performance in the history of baseball? Is it 41 wins? Three hundred eighty-three strikeouts? Sixteen shutouts? Is it 48 complete games? A 1.09 earned run average? A winning percentage of .947?

Baseball is now, always has been, and always will be a numbers game. But how does one equate Walter Johnson's 1.09 ERA in 1913 with Bob Gibson's 1.12 ERA 55 years later? How do we compare Jack Chesbro's 41 wins in 1904 with Denny McLain's 30 wins 64 years later?

The game has changed little in its more than 100 years, but pitching has changed drastically with today's penchant for five-man rotations, pitch counts, and the rise to prominence and importance of the relief pitcher, or "closer." Never again will we see a pitcher win 41 games in a season (we probably will never see a pitcher start 41 games in a season), or pitch 48 complete games in a season (in 2001, Roger Clemens became the first pitcher to win 20 games without pitching a single complete game).

There is no one around who has seen Cy Young pitch, or Christy Mathewson, or Walter Johnson, so we have only statistics by which to measure their performances. But the numbers become skewed when you compare those from the "dead ball" era, when entire teams hit fewer home runs than today's utility infielders, with those of the post–World War II era; or compare the pitchers of the forties, fifties, and sixties with those of the past two decades. Consequently, it behooves one to limit such comparisons to pitchers within the same era.

So with full disclosure that this is purely a subjective listing, we present the 10 greatest single-season pitching performances in baseball history:

1. Steve Carlton, 1972—On the surface, a record of 27–10 would not seem to merit such a lofty perch. Other pitchers have won more, and lost fewer. However, Carlton's record jumps out in comparison to his peers' and the team for which he pitched. The 1972 Philadelphia Phillies won 59 games, so Carlton won a phenomenal 46 percent of his team's games. No other pitcher in baseball history ever won such a preponderance of his team's games. He also pitched 70 percent of his team's complete games, 62 percent of his team's shutouts, and recorded 33 percent of his team's strikeouts.

> Carlton won a phenomenal 46 percent of his team's games. No other pitcher in baseball history ever won such a preponderance of his team's games. He also pitched 70 percent of his team's complete games, 62 percent of his team's shutouts, and recorded 33 percent of his team's strikeouts.

His 27 wins were six more than Tom Seaver. His 310 strikeouts were 61 more than Seaver. And his 30 complete games were seven more than Ferguson Jenkins.

2. Nolan Ryan, 1973—Ryan was only 21–16 with a 2.87 ERA, but he was five games over .500 for a team, the California Angels, that was four games under .500. The definitive number in Ryan's season was his record 383 strikeouts. They came in the first year of the designated hitter, meaning Ryan never pitched against a pitcher. If he had, he likely would have topped 400 strikeouts for the season. He also pitched two of his seven no-hitters in the 1973 season.

3. Grover Cleveland Alexander, 1916—"Old Pete" pitched a record 16 shutouts and 38 complete games. He won 33 games, had an ERA of 1.55, and led the National League in strikeouts with 167.

4. Bob Gibson, 1968—It was the "Year of the Pitcher." Denny McLain of the Detroit Tigers became the first pitcher in 34 years (Dizzy Dean, 1934) and the first American League pitcher in 37 years (Lefty Grove, 1931) to win 30 games; Juan Marichal won 26 games and completed 30 games; Don Drysdale set a record with 58 2/3 consecutive scoreless innings (since broken), and Gibson had the incredible earned run average of 1.12. He also led the National League with 268 strikeouts and 13 shutouts. It was hardly a surprise that Gibson won 22 games. The surprise was that he won *only* 22 games, and that he lost 9.

5. Jack Chesbro, 1904—Although he pitched in baseball's dark ages, and never has been mentioned among the game's greatest pitchers, there is no way to ignore Chesbro's 41 wins (he also lost 12 games) for the New York Highlanders (later the Yankees) in 1904. It's the most wins ever recorded by a pitcher in one season and one record that, safe to say, never will be broken. Chesbro started 51 times, 33 percent of his team's games, and pitched in relief in four others, recording three wins to top the 40 mark. He pitched a staggering 454 2/3 innings, completed a record 48 games, had an earned run average of 1.82, struck out 239 batters, and pitched six shutouts.

6. Sandy Koufax, 1965, 1966—Back-to-back seasons were practically a carbon copy of one another, so they are combined as the sixth best season for a pitcher. In 1965, Koufax was 26–8 with a 2.04 ERA, 27 complete games, 382 strikeouts (a record at the time), and eight shutouts. He then followed that up with a 27–9 record in 1966, lowered his ERA to 1.73, again completed 27 games, struck out 317, and pitched five shutouts. Although the 27 wins were the most of his career, Koufax stunned the baseball world by quitting after the

Bittersweet Memory

One would expect Ron Guidry to say his best game was when he struck out 18 California Angels in Yankee Stadium on the night of June 17, 1978. Certainly, it was the defining game of his career, a 4–0 four-hitter that raised his record to 14–0 on his way to his greatest season: a record of 25–3, an earned run average of 1.74, a league-leading nine shutouts, 248 strikeouts, plus a 2–0 record in the postseason.

"That's the game everybody wants to talk about," Guidry agreed. "But I don't consider it the best game I ever pitched. The 18-strikeout game was a personal gratification thing because you don't get to stand up on the mound very often and just strike out people at will. You have to have a lot of lucky things happen in a game like that. Guys have to take pitches when they should be swinging, and swing when they should be taking.

"I didn't usually strike out many hitters on called strikes. That was just one of those nights. I'd start a hitter off with a breaking ball and he'd swing at a ball in the dirt. The next time he'd be taking the first pitch and I'd throw a fastball right down the middle of the plate and he'd take it. You're fortunate because that's how that night went. A lot of other times, you might throw that same fastball and they'd way-lay it because that's what they're guessing. That night was just one of those special nights where every time they guessed, it was wrong."

The game Guidry considers his best also came against the Angels, this time in Anaheim, a 1–0 loss to Nolan Ryan on May 2, 1979.

"What made that game special was the magnitude of the guys pitching in the game because it came after my good year," Guidry said. "It was a 5:30 game, and it was a case of the guy who loses out-pitches the other guy and still he loses." Guidry gave up five hits, Ryan six; Guidry struck out nine, Ryan seven. As Guidry explained:

I lost the game on a fly-ball double because the hitter [infielder Jim Anderson] was a young kid who was playing because somebody was hurt and we didn't know him. So they moved [left fielder] Lou Piniella over toward center field because they didn't think the kid would pull the ball. So he pulled it to left and it fell in for a double. If Lou had been playing a regular left field, it would have been caught.

Nolan went out about the fifth inning, and he didn't take any warm-up pitches. He just pointed to the catcher as if to say, "Let's go," and I'm sitting in the dugout and I'm thinking, "What is this?" So when I went out for the next inning, I didn't take any warm-ups. I just pointed to Thurman [Munson] and said, "Let's go."

It was a very fast game [two hours and two minutes]. I was sitting in the dugout when Nolan got the last out [Mickey Rivers on a ground ball to first baseman Rod Carew]. His teammates went out to congratulate Nolan and I picked up my stuff and started to walk to the locker room. When I got to the end of our dugout, Nolan was in front of his dugout and he turned and looked at me and took off his cap. I waved to him and gave him a "thumbs up."

That was special. That's something that doesn't happen often. I've pitched against other pitchers and we usually didn't acknowledge the job that we did. It was fun going through the lineup, boom . . . boom . . . boom. . . . Other than the run they scored in the third inning, the game was easy for both of us. It wasn't fun to lose the game, but it was fun in the sense that you competed and gave it everything, and you lost 1–0.

I saw Nolan in the outfield the next day and I went over to him, shook his hand, and said, "I didn't want to lose, but I didn't mind losing." And he said, "It's a game none of us should have lost. I was fortunate that I came out on top, but I wouldn't have minded losing 1–0 to you." That's special. You're not going to get that very often.

Guidry, it seemed, could do no wrong during his magical 1978 season, compiling a 25–3 record and a 1.74 ERA for the world-champion Yankees.

1966 season because of an arthritic elbow. At the time, he was at the top of his game and had not yet turned 31 years old.

7. Walter Johnson, 1913—No pitcher in history so outdistanced his competition as the great "Big Train." This was his greatest season and his numbers dwarfed every other American League pitcher. The dominant strikeout pitcher of his era, Johnson struck out 243 batters in 1913, 77 more than the league's number two man. He led the league with 36 wins, 13 more than the runner-up, with an earned run average of 1.09, the best in baseball's so-called "modern era," in complete games with 29, and in shutouts with 11. Also, as a sign of the times, he helped himself at bat, hitting .261 with five doubles, six triples, two home runs, and 14 runs batted in.

8. Ron Guidry, 1978, and Dwight Gooden, 1985—Their records are comparable, it would be impossible to separate them. If there is one overriding difference, it's that Gooden accomplished his big season at the age of 20. Guidry was 27 in 1978, but in only his second full major league season when he was 25–3, an .893 winning percentage, for the Yankees. Gooden was 24–4, an .857 winning percentage, for the Mets in 1985. Guidry had nine shutouts to Gooden's eight, and both had 16 complete games. Gooden had a slightly better earned run average (1.53 to 1.74), and more strikeouts (268 to 248), but Guidry had an 18-strikeout game.

9. Ed Walsh, 1908, and Christy Mathewson, 1908—Once again, it's impossible to separate two almost identical performances, even more difficult because both came in the same year, albeit in different leagues. Another similarity is how Walsh, of the Chicago White Sox, and Mathewson, the "Big Six" of the New York Giants, far outdistanced their rivals.

Aside from Jack Chesbro in 1904, "Big Ed" Walsh is the only pitcher in the modern (post-1903) era to win 40 games (Charles "Old Hoss" Radbourn won 60 in 1884). Walsh was 40–15 in 1908, a winning percentage of .727, and won 16 games more than any other American League pitcher. Mathewson was 37–11, a winning percentage of .771, and won eight games more than any other National League pitcher. Walsh had a 1.42 ERA to Mathewson's 1.43, 42 complete games to Matty's 34, and 269 strikeouts to Mathewson's 259. Matty pitched 12 shutouts, one more than Walsh.

10. Lefty Grove, 1931—The last American Leaguer to win 30 games before Denny McLain 37 years later, Grove was 31–4 in 1931 with a 2.06 earned run average, 27 complete games, 175 strikeouts, and four shutouts.

Although they failed to make the cut, the following single-season performances are worthy of mention:

Dizzy Dean, 1934—The last National League pitcher to win 30 games, Dean was 30–7 for the St. Louis Cardinals' Gashouse Gang, a winning percentage of .811. He led the league in complete games with 24, strikeouts with 195, and shutouts with 11.

Bob Feller, 1946—After missing three and a half seasons because of military service, Feller returned to dominate the American League in 1946 with a record of 26–15, a 2.18 earned run average, 36 complete games, 10 shutouts, including the second of his three no-hitters, and 348 strikeouts.

Elroy Face, 1959—Pitching exclusively in relief for the Pittsburgh Pirates, Face was 18–1 and recorded the highest single-season winning percentage in history, .947. He also saved 10 games.

Whitey Ford, 1961—Put on a four-man rotation by manager Ralph Houk, Ford was a 20-game winner for the first time in his career. He was 25–4, a

Tom Terrific

Three hundred and eleven wins, 3,640 strikeouts, 61 shutouts, a no-hitter, a 19-strikeout game that he ended by striking out the last 10 hitters. Tom Seaver did it all in a 20-year Hall of Fame career.

Asked to choose his greatest game, Seaver was in a quandary. He had a laundry list of games from which to choose:

• His 300th win. It came at Yankee Stadium on Sunday afternoon, August 4, 1985, while a member of the Chicago White Sox. Seaver beat the Yankees 4–1, with a complete-game six-hitter. He walked one and struck out seven. "That was my most memorable game, not my best," he said.

• His no-hitter. Pitching for the Cincinnati Reds on June16, 1978, Seaver beat the St. Louis Cardinals 4–0, at Riverfront Stadium. He walked three and struck out three.

• His 19-strikeout game. It came at Shea Stadium on April 22, 1970, while pitching for the New York Mets, a complete-game, two-hit, 2–1 victory over the San Diego Padres. Seaver walked one.

• His near-perfect game. Seaver calls it his "Imperfect Game." On July 9, 1969, at Shea Stadium, Seaver retired the first 25 Chicago Cubs. With one out in the ninth, a journeyman outfielder named Jimmy Qualls, who would get just 31 hits in a 63-game major league career, lined a single to center. It would be the Cubs' only hit, their only base runner. Seaver walked none and struck out 11 in a 4–0 win.

Which does Seaver consider his greatest game? None of the above.

"It's a difficult choice," Seaver admits, "but I think the best game I ever pitched was against the Dodgers in Los Angeles. I left after 12 innings, tied 1–1."

He eliminated the no-hitter because he didn't feel his stuff was dominant (note the three strikeouts), and the 19-strikeout game because "I had a 2–1 lead and the shadows helped me get some of those strikeouts."

The choice, therefore, came down to Seaver's "Imperfect Game," and a game he pitched for the Mets on Wednesday, May 1, 1974, at Dodger Stadium, and Seaver opted for the latter. He and Andy Messersmith dueled through 11 innings, tied 1–1. Seaver would leave after pitching the twelfth, and the Dodgers won, 2–1, with a run in the bottom of the fourteenth.

"I made one bad pitch the entire game," Seaver said. "A hanging slider to [Steve] Garvey and he hit it out. Every other pitch I was able to put exactly where I wanted it. In the 'Imperfect Game,' I also was able to put every pitch where I wanted it. What happened there is that Qualls was a hitter I didn't know. I had never faced him, and he hit the ball hard three times."

On May 1, 1974, Seaver held the Dodgers hitless until Garvey homered leading off the fifth. The Mets tied the score on Wayne Garrett's leadoff home run in the top of the eighth, and that's where they stood when Seaver left after 12 innings. He allowed just three hits—Garvey's homer, an infield single by Bill Russell in the eighth, and a single by Bill Buckner in the twelfth. Seaver ended the inning, and his night's work, by striking out Garvey for the third time—Seaver's 16th strikeout of the game.

CHAPTER 24

Seaver, beaming after his 25th win of the 1969 season, put the Miracle Mets on his back to commandeer one of the greatest rags-to-riches stories in baseball history. However, his most memorable game, at least in his own opinion, came in 1974.

winning percentage of .862. He then followed up his best regular season with two wins and a 0.00 ERA in the World Series, while raising his World Series consecutive scoreless innings streak to 32, breaking the record set in 1918 by Babe Ruth.

Tom Seaver, 1969—His 25–7 record, 2.21 earned run average, 18 complete games, 208 strikeouts, and five shutouts enabled the Miracle New York Mets to jump from ninth place in 1968 to their first world championship in 1969.

Mike Marshall, 1974—At a time when there was no such thing as a "closer," and relief pitchers often worked two, three, and four innings, Marshall appeared in a record 106 games for the Los Angeles Dodgers, pitched 208 innings, won 15 games, and saved 21 others.

Roger Clemens, 1986—A 24–4 record, 2.48 earned run average, 10 complete games, and 238 strikeouts earned him the first of six Cy Young Awards and was the best season in the career of the 300-game winner.

It is safe to say that Chesbro's numbers for the 1904 season—41 victories and 48 complete games—are in the record books to stay.

The Ryan Express

No pitcher in baseball history, when asked to choose the greatest game he ever pitched, has as many choices as Nolan Ryan. Was it one of his seven no-hitters, almost twice as many as any other pitcher (Sandy Koufax is second with four)—the last at the age of 44 years, three months, and one day? Was it his 19-strikeout game? Was it one of the two games in which he struck out the side in an inning with just nine pitches?

Ryan's choice?

None of the above. He opted for a game he pitched for the California Angels against the Boston Red Sox in Anaheim Stadium on Sunday, July 9, 1972.

Ryan started the game by walking Red Sox leadoff hitter Tommy Harper. After Doug Griffin struck out, Ryan faced Carl Yastrzemski, who, according to Nolan, "rolled a ball in the hole between the shortstop and second baseman into right field. We had the shift on, everybody pulled over to the right, and Yastrzemski hit a slow roller that just got through the infield. I retired the next 26 batters."

That's only part of the story. After Yaz's hit, Ryan struck out Reggie Smith and Rico Petrocelli to end the inning. In the second, he fanned Carlton Fisk, Bob Burda, and Juan Beniquez. In the third, he struck out Sonny Siebert, Harper, and Griffin, giving him eight consecutive strike-outs, an American League record that he accomplished twice.

Ryan and Siebert dueled through three scoreless innings until the Angels scored three in the fourth. And that's how it ended: a 3–0 California victory.

It was one of 12 one-hitters in Ryan's career, and it came within inches of being his eighth no-hitter. He walked one and struck out sixteen, getting at least one strikeout in every inning except the fourth, and striking out every Red Sox player except Yastrzemski once (he got Fisk three times). It was one of 26 times in his career that Ryan struck out 15 or more batters in a game, and one of 215 times that he struck out at least 10 in a game.

"That was as overpowering a game as I've ever pitched," Ryan said. "More overpowering than the no-hitters."

Bobby Thigpen, 1990—No relief pitcher had saved 50 games until Thigpen raised the bar by saving 57 for the Chicago White Sox. He also won four and had a 1.83 earned run average. He never saved more than 34 games in any of his other eight major league seasons.

Dennis Eckersley, 1990—In the same year Thigpen saved 57, and in the same league, Eckersley saved 48 games for the Oakland Athletics. But he had an ERA of 0.61 and walked only four batters in 73 1/3 innings.

Randy Johnson, 2002—A record of 24–5, a 2.32 ERA, four shutouts, 334 strikeouts, and his fifth Cy Young award.

Pedro Martinez, 2002—Cy Young voters chose Barry Zito over Martinez, who was 20–4 with a 2.26 ERA and 239 strikeouts.

Ryan set the single-season strikeout mark in 1973 with 383 Ks, a number that likely would have surpassed 400 had it not been for the designated hitter rule.

Carlton's Cy Young Award season of 1972 (his first of four Cys) was particularly remarkable because he dominated opposing lineups while pitching for a team that won a mere 59 games that year.

Johnson, the dominant pitcher of his era—and among the greatest of all time in most experts' opinions—
had his finest season ever, including a "modern-record" 1.09 ERA, in 1913.

Curveballs in the Mist

Sandy Koufax should throw perfect games. Cy Young should throw one. David Cone was not a huge surprise. We'll even give you Catfish Hunter.

But Len Barker? Putting the Nuke Laloosh wannabe with those immortals is like drinking light beer with caviar. But he did it . . . Barker joined the pantheon with his unhittable, perfect performance on a misty night in Cleveland's old, barnlike Municipal Stadium.

Ironically, Barker nearly missed his one shot at history. He was running late getting to the ballpark because he had gone to the airport to pick up his visiting brother. Who would have thought, when he rushed into the locker room barely an hour before game time, that he would be carried off by the end of it?

Barker came into that game on a hot streak that had started in 1980 when he led the AL with 187 strikeouts. A big man at 6'5" and more than 220 pounds, he was a power pitcher who relied on his fastball to do most of the heavy lifting. But like *Bull Durham*'s Laloosh, he often combined wildness with wildfire, also leading the league with 92 walks in 1980. "Going into a game, you sort of expected Lenny to walk a few batters," his catcher Ron Hassey said.

Barker admits being rushed in his pregame prep, and before he knew it, he was on the hill, a heavy mist enveloping the park as he got set to face the Toronto Blue Jays. "The misty conditions helped me rub the ball up better," he said in a 2001 interview. "The water helped me rub them up where I got a really good grip that wouldn't slip, and that gave me better rotation on my curveball." As it turned out, that curveball became what *Sports Illustrated*'s Bruce Newman called a "God-given spitter."

Hassey said that the curve Barker had that night was the best he'd ever seen him throw. The batterymates realized that fact early and changed Barker's ratio from 90 percent fastballs to more than 60 percent curves.

While Barker was racking up what would end up being a total of 11 strikeouts (third most to Koufax in a perfect game), most on that wet, wicked curve, he got some help from the Indians defense. Alfredo Griffin,

> "The water helped me rub them up where I got a really good grip that wouldn't slip, and that gave me better rotation on my curveball."
> —Len Barker

the very first batter, in fact, hit a slow roller that shortstop Tom Veryzer had to charge and field bare-handed. Center fielder Rick Manning tracked down a long fly by Damaso Garcia in the second. Then in the fifth, Toby Harrah went into the seats along third base to snag Willie Upshaw's high, twisting foul pop. Accounts of the game have called that catch unbelievable.

By then Barker led 2–0, and in the stands, his wife, Bonnie, and brother, Chuck, were getting nervous. "I am so superstitious," Bonnie Barker said. "I was thinking about it from the fifth inning on, but I tried to blank it out of my mind." Duane Kuiper made a nice play in the seventh, going to his left to get another grounder by Griffin.

Barker kept breaking off curves and mowing them down. In the ninth, with whomever was still left from the seven thousand–plus crowd now on their feet, Barker got Ernie Whitt to fly to Manning in center to end it.

"I would have run to the pitcher's mound to catch that one," Manning said. He also got permission to keep that final ball, and it remains to this day on his mantelpiece.

"To tell you the honest truth," Barker said of the postgame mob scene, "I didn't know if it was a perfect game until someone out there told me."

The clubhouse guy greeted him soon after with the "white-carpet" treatment, a trail of towels leading to his locker and a six-pack arranged like a zero. That evening, when Bonnie and Len finally arrived home, they found their garage covered with signs and posters from the neighbors.

To this day, Barker is upbeat and thrilled to talk about this one special night. He's the sort of athlete who realizes just what an honor it was to not only play baseball for a living, but to have done something that will live in history.

Unfortunately, it is the nature of baseball fate that such lightning strikes but once. Though he enjoyed several more productive seasons before arm trouble forced him into the construction business, Barker never again found that magical combination of moisture and moment.

"I never found that curveball again after that game. And I've been looking for 20 years."

Barker found some time before the next day's game to read congratulatory telegrams after his perfect game in Cleveland.

LEN BARKER'S PERFECT GAME
MAY 15, 1981

Toronto	AB	R	H	RBI
Griffin, ss	3	0	0	0
Moseby, rf	3	0	0	0
Bell, lf	3	0	0	0
Mayberry, 1b	3	0	0	0
Upshaw, dh	3	0	0	0
Garcia, 2b	3	0	0	0
Bosetti, cf	3	0	0	0
Ainge, 3b	2	0	0	0
Woods, ph	1	0	0	0
Martinez, c	2	0	0	0
Whitt, ph	1	0	0	0
Leal, p	0	0	0	0
Totals	**27**	**0**	**0**	**0**

Cleveland	AB	R	H	RBI
Manning, cf	4	1	1	0
Orta, rf	4	1	3	1
Hargrove, 1b	4	1	1	0
Thornton, dh	3	0	0	1
Hassey, c	4	0	1	1
Harrah, 3b	4	0	1	0
Charboneau, lf	3	0	0	0
Kuiper, 2b	3	0	0	0
Veryzer, ss	3	0	0	0
Barker, p	0	0	0	0
Totals	**32**	**3**	**7**	**3**

	1	2	3	4	5	6	7	8	9	R	H	E
Tor	0	0	0	0	0	0	0	0	0	0	0	3
Cle	2	0	0	0	0	0	0	1	x	3	7	0

Toronto	IP	H	R	ER	BB	K
Leal (L)	8	7	3	1	0	5

Cleveland	IP	H	R	ER	BB	K
Barker (W)	9	0	0	0	0	11

Time—2:09; Att.—7,290

Family Affair

Bonnie Barker and Chuck Barker weren't the only ones in the family to enjoy this special moment.

Len Barker's father-in-law regularly tuned in to hear Barker's games. A strong signal let him hear Indians broadcasts all the way in Norristown, Pennsylvania. But the weather was playing tricks with the reception. He hopped in his car and drove to a golf course near his house and listened to history sitting in the front seat while the rain peppered the roof like long-distance applause.

Barker's mom, Emogene McCurry, was listening, too, all the way in Philadelphia. However, she lost the signal in the eighth.

Left to Barker's 92-year-old grandmother Tokie Lockhart is this classic coda to the Len Barker story: "Tell Len I'm very proud of him, and I hope he does better next time."

A Perfect Ending

For the 1984 California Angels and Texas Rangers teams, it was an ending. The long, hot summer was coming to a close. With this game, their seasons would end. For some, this would be an ending of another sort: a final game, a final moment in the sun.

For Angels pitcher Mike Witt, however, it was a beginning. As he threw the final pitch of what would become the first and only perfect game in Angels history, Witt began a journey that would make him successful and rich. For him, the experience of pitching a perfect game not only thrilled and enlivened him, it improved him. For some pitchers, a perfect game is a pinnacle, and it was certainly so for Witt, but the view from the mountaintop for him just showed other mountains waiting to be climbed.

The game was played on the final day of the 1984 season in a hot and quiet Arlington Stadium. Both teams were playing out the string, their bags packed for a quick postgame getaway to winter. Until a few days earlier, the Angels were still in the AL West race, but that possibility had fallen by the wayside, and now the goal was to finish and go home.

"It was about as meaningless a game as you could imagine," remembered writer Tim Kurkjian, now of ESPN but then covering the game for the *Dallas Morning News*. "It was a Sunday afternoon in Texas and the Cowboys were playing at the same time." In fact, the next day's *Dallas Times-Herald* carried their story of the game along the bottom of the front sports page, well below several Cowboys articles.

Witt was sharp early, making leadoff hitter Mickey Rivers the first of his 10 strikeout victims on the day. In the second, he got some help when third baseman Doug DeCinces charged a topper by Larry Parrish; DeCinces' off-balance throw nipped Parrish.

While Witt continued to put up zeroes, his opponents realized early on that he had special stuff that day. "His stuff was awesome," said opposing pitcher Charlie Hough, who ended up allowing no earned runs and only seven hits himself. "I'd seen other no-hitters and this was the most overpowering."

Witt's teammate Mike Brown, who would play a key defensive role later, was aware of it, too, having gotten the hit that broke up Britt Burns' near-perfect game a year earlier. "I was aware of what Mike was doing by about the fourth inning," Brown remembers.

However, the press box was less aware. Even Hall of Fame *Los Angeles Times* writer Ross Newhan remembers that "it snuck up on us. We were all

packed and ready to go to Kansas City for the playoffs. I hate to say this, but you kind of rooted against the guy so you don't have to do another story on getaway day."

He wasn't the only writer rooting for a Texas hit. Another Angels beat writer had skipped the game to fly ahead for playoff coverage. Tom Singer relied on his pal Kurkjian and wire-service copy to help him file for the *Orange County Register*.

The story might have been different for all those writers, as the Angels were having trouble getting Witt the run he needed to seal the deal. Finally, they broke through in the seventh. DeCinces scored on a Reggie Jackson fielder's choice; the run was unearned because of an earlier passed ball.

In the top of the eighth, Brown saved the day for Witt, chasing down a long fly out to right center by Parrish. "When Larry hit it, I thought it had home-run possibility," Witt said afterward. "Then I thought it had wall possibility. Then when Mike got there, I saw it had glove possibility."

"I didn't care if I hit that wall going full speed," says Brown. "There was no way I was not going to catch that ball."

The ninth came and with it came Witt's first butterflies. "I was as nervous going out for the ninth as I was for my first pro start," he said. Also nervous was his wife, Lisa, along for the season's final road trip. "I thought about the no-hitter from about the fifth inning," she says. "But I had never even heard of a perfect game!"

Angels manager John McNamara gave Witt some extra help by creating a ninth-inning outfield of Fred Lynn, Gary Pettis, and veteran gloveman Derrel Thomas. Having thrown less than 90 pitches heading into the ninth, Witt was fresh as a daisy, too.

Tommy Dunbar looked at two curveballs and then fanned on a fastball. Bobby Jones, pinch hitting, grounded out.

Marv Foley pinch hit, and in the final at-bat of his major league career, smacked a grounder to Rob Wilfong at second, and Mike Witt entered history.

Witt's teammates mobbed him at the mound, leading him into what would end up being a brief clubhouse celebration . . . they had a flight to catch, after all. Witt spent so much time enjoying the moment that he had to find a helpful Texas fan to drive the Witts' rental car back to the airport. "I didn't know what else to do, so I gave him the keys. And he actually did return it!"

With the NFL season in full swing and the playoffs two days away, Witt's perfecto did not get the same sort of ongoing press that other games enjoyed. Witt, however, took away something more important than a *Good*

> "His stuff was awesome. I'd seen other no-hitters and this was the most overpowering."
> —Charlie Hough

MIKE WITT'S PERFECT GAME
SEPTEMBER 30, 1984

California	AB	R	H	RBI
Wilfong, 2b	4	0	0	0
Sconiers, 1b	3	0	0	0
Grich, 1b	0	0	0	0
Lynn, cf	4	0	2	0
DeCinces, 3b	4	1	2	0
Downing, lf	4	0	0	0
Thomas, lf	0	0	0	0
Jackson, dh	4	0	0	1
Brown, rf	3	0	3	0
Pettis, cf	0	0	0	0
Boone, c	3	0	0	0
Schofield, ss	2	0	0	0
Totals	**31**	**1**	**7**	**1**

Texas	AB	R	H	RBI
Rivers, dh	3	0	0	0
Tolleson, 2b	3	0	0	0
Ward, lf	3	0	0	0
Parrish, 3b	3	0	0	0
O'Brien, 1b	3	0	0	0
Wright, cf	3	0	0	0
Dunbar, rf	3	0	0	0
Scott, c	2	0	0	0
Jones, ph	1	0	0	0
Wilkerson, ss	2	0	0	0
Foley, ph	1	0	0	0
Totals	**27**	**0**	**0**	**0**

	1	2	3	4	5	6	7	8	9	R	H	E
Cal	0	0	0	0	0	0	1	0	0	1	7	0
Tex	0	0	0	0	0	0	0	0	0	0	0	0

California	IP	H	R	ER	BB	K
Witt (W)	9	0	0	0	0	10

Texas	IP	H	R	ER	BB	K
Hough (L)	9	7	1	0	3	3

Time—1:49; Att.—8,375

The fanfare for Witt was relatively short-lived because his moment happened on the final day of the 1984 season.

Morning America clip. Witt credits the success of that one day with propelling him upward. He did win 15 that season, and was third in the league with 223 strikeouts, but that was his first good season. Following up on perfection, he had four straight seasons with double digits in wins, two All-Star selections, an AL West Division title in 1986, and a couple of good (and highly paid) years with the Yankees. Though injuries curtailed his career (he retired in 1993), that day remains a jumping-off point.

"I think I was always trying to figure out a way to find what I had that day again," he says thoughtfully. "But I realized that maybe I should start also thinking like an ace. No-hitters and games like I pitched are for the staff aces, I thought. Pitching this game gave me confidence, a real boost. Afterward, when I was in a slump, I would watch that game to figure out what I had done right that day. It was like trying to chase a rabbit with a greyhound . . . you'd never quite catch up to it. But that will always be special to me. It was a once-in-a-lifetime event and it really launched me into some good years."

Perfection can, for a pitcher, be a goal, an endpoint, the peak. For some pitchers, though, it is the first stop on a long and happy road.

Great Scott

For four years when he was a member of the New York Mets, knowledgeable and experienced baseball people kept waiting for Mike Scott to realize his enormous potential. When he finally fulfilled that promise years later in Houston, he was accused of cheating.

Scott was drafted by the Mets out of Pepperdine University in the June 1976 free agent draft. Three years later, he arrived in Shea Stadium, a young pitcher with a great arm and unlimited potential. But after he won 14 games and lost 27 in four seasons, the Mets grew tired of waiting for Scott to blossom and shipped him off to the Astros in exchange for journeyman outfielder Danny Heep.

Scott has said it was the change of scenery that caused his transformation, but more likely it was an encounter with pitching guru Roger Craig, an encounter arranged by Astros general manager Al Rosen.

After posting a 10–6 record in 1983, Scott slipped to 5–11, so Rosen sought out Craig and asked him to work with the young right-hander. As pitching coach for Sparky Anderson in Detroit, Craig had perfected a new pitch—the split-finger fastball—a variation of the old forkball, which he taught to Tigers pitchers and, generously, to any other pitcher disposed to learning the new pitch.

Scott spent a week in San Diego, an hour a day, working with Craig, soaking up all the information and technique he could. With his new pitch, Scott won 18 games in 1985 and found himself the center of a firestorm of controversy, accused of scuffing the baseball. Ironically, it was his tutor, Craig, and his former team, the Mets, who were most vociferous in their charges.

By 1986, Scott was a full-fledged star, hailed as one of the best pitchers in the National League, the ace of what Houston chroniclers regard as the best Astros team in their history. They started quickly and outdistanced the field in the National League West under rookie manager Hal Lanier.

On the afternoon of September 25, when they faced the Giants, managed by Scott's mentor and tormentor, Roger Craig, the Astros needed one win to clinch the second division championship in their 25 years. They had their ace, Scott, a 17-game winner, on the mound, and an expectant crowd of 32,808 in the Astrodome.

"I can't ever remember a game of such importance that was so dominated by one person."
—Nolan Ryan

The game started inauspiciously for Scott, whose first pitch hit Dan Gladden in the back. But he retired Robbie Thompson, Will Clark, and Candy Maldonado in order to put the Giants down.

Houston broke a scoreless tie in the fifth on a home run by Denny Walling, and added a run in the seventh on a single by Billy Doran, a wild pitch, and an RBI single by Jose Cruz.

Meanwhile, the Giants were helpless against Scott, who retired 19 Giants in a row from the second inning to the eighth. The only thing even close to a hit for the Giants came with one out and a runner on first in the eighth when Doran ranged far to his right for a shot up the middle and forced the runner at second.

"I started thinking about a no-hitter in the seventh," said Scott. "[Astros catcher Alan] Ashby told me, 'We're clinching the pennant anyway, just concentrate on the no-hitter.'"

In the ninth, Scott struck out Gladden and Thompson, his 12th and 13th strikeouts, and faced Clark, the Giants' best hitter, for the final out. Clark hit a weak grounder to first baseman Glenn Davis, who grabbed it and stepped on first for the final out of a 2–0 Astros' win and the NL West title.

Scott had pitched the only no-hitter in baseball history that clinched a championship (Allie Reynolds' second no-hitter of the season for the Yankees 35 years earlier had clinched a tie for the American League pennant).

"If he's not the Cy Young Award winner, then I've never seen one," said Scott's Astros teammate Nolan Ryan, already the author of five no-hitters himself. "I can't ever remember a game of such importance that was so dominated by one person."

In his next start, Scott challenged Johnny Vander Meer's 48-year-old record of two consecutive no-hitters. He pitched five perfect innings against the Giants and took his second consecutive no-hitter into the seventh inning, when it was broken up by Clark's leadoff double.

After winning their division, the Astros faced their expansion brothers, the Mets, in the National League Championship Series with a chance to go to the World Series for the first time in franchise history.

In Game 1 of the best-of-seven series, Scott beat Doc Gooden, 1–0, on a five-hitter, striking out 14. The Mets came back to win Games 2 and 3, but Scott again dominated the Mets in Game 4, beating Sid Fernandez, 3–1, on a three-hitter to tie the series at two games apiece.

The Mets won Game 5, 2–1, in 12 innings to go up three games to two, but their worst fears were that if they failed to win Game 6 and had

Scott (center) clinched the 1986 N.L. West title in spectacular fashion.

MIKE SCOTT'S NO-HITTER
SEPTEMBER 25, 1986

San Francisco	AB	R	H	RBI
Gladden, cf	3	0	0	0
Thompson, 2b	4	0	0	0
Clark, 1b	4	0	0	0
Maldonado, lf	3	0	0	0
C. Davis, rf	2	0	0	0
Brenly, 3b	3	0	0	0
Ouellette, c	2	0	0	0
Uribe, ss	2	0	0	0
Spilman, ph	1	0	0	0
Quinones, ss	0	0	0	0
Berenguer, p	0	0	0	0
Lancellotti, ph	1	0	0	0
M. Davis, p	0	0	0	0
Aldrete, ph	1	0	0	0
Garrelts, p	0	0	0	0
Totals	**27**	**0**	**0**	**0**

Houston	AB	R	H	RBI
Hatcher, cf	4	0	0	0
Doran, 2b	4	0	2	0
Walling, 3b	4	2	2	1
G. Davis, 1b	2	0	1	0
Bass, rf	3	0	1	0
Cruz, lf	2	0	1	1
Ashby, c	4	0	2	0
Reynolds, ss	2	0	0	0
Thon, ss	2	0	0	0
Scott, p	4	0	1	0
Totals	**31**	**2**	**10**	**2**

	1	2	3	4	5	6	7	8	9	R	H	E
SanF	0	0	0	0	0	0	0	0	0	0	10	0
Hou	0	0	0	0	1	0	1	0	x	2	0	0

San Francisco	IP	H	R	ER	BB	K
Berenguer (L)	5	8	1	1	4	2
M. Davis	2	2	1	1	1	3
Garrelts	1	0	0	0	0	3

Houston	IP	H	R	ER	BB	K
Scott (W)	9	0	0	0	2	13

Time—2:24; Att.—32,808

to go to a sudden-death seventh game, they would be facing Scott, who in two games had held them to one run and eight hits, walked one, and struck out 19.

Many have called Game 6 of the 1986 NLCS the greatest game ever played. The Astros scored three runs in the first, and the score remained 3–0 until the top of the ninth when the Mets, with the specter of Mike Scott looming on their horizon, rallied to tie and force extra innings. The Mets scored a run in the top of the fourteenth, and the Astros tied it in the bottom of the fourteenth on a home run by Billy Hatcher.

The Mets scored three in the top of the sixteenth. Undaunted, the Astros came back to score two in the bottom of the sixteenth. With two outs and two runners on base, Jesse Orosco fanned Kevin Bass to give the Mets a 7–6 win and their third National League pennant, depriving Scott of one more shot at his old team and a chance to pitch the Astros into their first World Series.

While the season ended in disappointment and frustration for the Astros and their fans, almost two decades later, Mike Scott's no-hitter on September 25, 1986, which clinched the National League West championship, remains the signature game in Houston baseball history.

Scott enjoyed one of the more dominant stretches by a pitcher in modern history late in the 1986 season and into the NLCS.

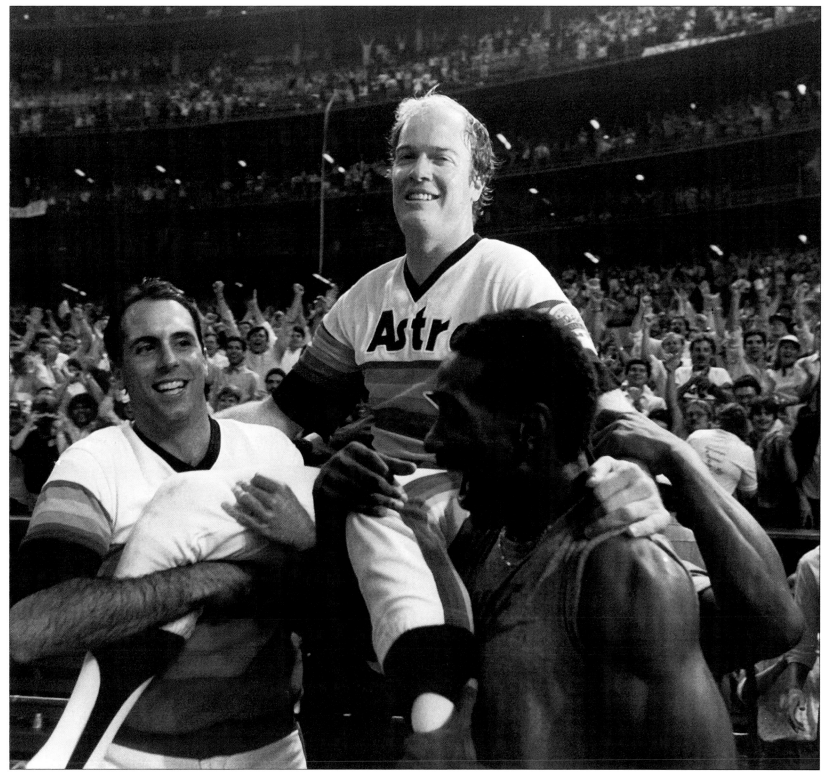

Despite Scott's division-clinching no-hitter and heroics in the playoffs, his Astros fell excruciatingly short of their first trip to the World Series.

Cruise Control

Before and after the Cincinnati Reds' 1–0 victory over the Dodgers on September 16, 1988, pitcher Tom Browning was all wet.

Before the game, it was from rain. . . . Afterward, it was from champagne.

After waiting out a 2-hour, 27-minute rain delay, Browning became only the third left-hander ever to throw a perfect game. He was also the only one to do it against a team that would go on to win the World Series the same year.

The Dodgers led the Reds by seven games going into that game, so Cincinnati still maintained some distant hope of the playoffs. But the rain delay took some of the edge off their enthusiasm, it seemed, and neither team had a hit through five innings. In the sixth, though, Barry Larkin touched Tim Belcher for a double. Chris Sabo hit a high bouncer to Jeff Hamilton at third, but his throw got by first baseman Mickey Hatcher, and Larkin scored. It would prove to be the only run. (Browning joined four other perfect-game pitchers who got their only run or runs via errors by the other team.)

For his part, Browning was eliminating Dodgers in a ruthlessly routine manner. "It was over before we knew it," remembered his catcher, Jeff Reed. "When Tom was pitching well, you tried to keep him in rhythm, so I just got the ball back to him quickly and let him go."

In the eighth, soon-to-be World Series hero Kirk Gibson earned a perfect-game asterisk, becoming the first player kicked out of one. Years later, he was still grumbling, "The strike zone was ridiculous. Not to take anything away from either pitcher, because it was a well-played game. But when the plate gets too big, it's hard to handle."

Reds broadcaster Marty Brennaman was finding it hard to handle for a different reason. "A lot of guys have been calling games for a long time and never had one. This was my first, and I was so nervous I could hardly keep my scorebook."

Reds manager Pete Rose told Reed to make sure Browning didn't work *too* fast. "Don't let him rush," Rose said. "Sometimes when he is going good, he throws a first-pitch fastball right down Broadway."

But not even Reed could slow the pace of the game. "The game went so quickly," he remembers. "With Belcher pitching so well, too. Before you knew it, it was the ninth inning."

A Pair of Three-peats

Paul O'Neill played right field for Browning that night in Cincinnati. When he later was part of the perfect games thrown by David Wells and David Cone, O'Neill became the only player ever to play on the winning side in three perfect games.

Alfredo Griffin, the Dodgers' shortstop that night, had already lost to Len Barker in 1981 while with Toronto and would go on to lose with the Dodgers against Dennis Martinez in 1991. He thus holds the dubious record of being the only player on the losing side of three perfect games.

> "It was over before we knew it. When Tom was pitching well, you tried to keep him in rhythm, so I just got the ball back to him quickly and let him go."
> —Reds catcher Jeff Reed

After two quick outs in the ninth, Browning was in the same position as another Reds pitcher had been earlier that season. Ron Robinson had become one of only six pitchers to lose a perfect game with two outs in the ninth. Browning himself had lost a no-hitter with one out in the ninth in a June game against the Padres.

But this time he finished it off, striking out Tracy Woodson on a head-high fastball to end it. It was perhaps the most routine and drama-free of any perfect game. It just seemed to sort of . . . happen.

Browning reflected later on what had made the difference. "Sometimes I lost my concentration in games and made bad pitches. But that night, I never lost it. I was in complete control of the strike zone. I never lost it."

Following Woodson's K, Reed remembers, "We just piled on! I remember me and Tom were on the bottom of the pile."

"Somebody actually split my lip in the pileup there," Browning said. So add a little blood to the list of liquids for Browning that night. But the champagne was the sweetest tasting of all.

Browning was in the driver's seat from the opening pitch of his perfect game in 1988.

TOM BROWNING'S PERFECT GAME
SEPTEMBER 16, 1988

Los Angeles	AB	R	H	RBI
Griffin, ss	3	0	0	0
Hatcher, 1b	3	0	0	0
Gibson, lf	3	0	0	0
Gonzalez, lf	0	0	0	0
Marshall, rf	3	0	0	0
Shelby, cf	3	0	0	0
Hamilton, 3b	3	0	0	0
Dempsey, c	3	0	0	0
Sax, 2b	3	0	0	0
Belcher, p	2	0	0	0
Woodson, ph	1	0	0	0
Totals	**27**	**0**	**0**	**0**

Cincinnati	AB	R	H	RBI
Larkin, ss	3	1	1	0
Sabo, 3b	3	0	1	0
Daniels, lf	3	0	0	0
Davis, cf	2	0	0	0
O'Neill, rf	3	0	0	0
Esasky, 1b	3	0	0	0
Reed, c	3	0	0	0
Oester, 2b	3	0	1	0
Browning, p	3	0	0	0
Totals	**26**	**1**	**3**	**0**

	1	2	3	4	5	6	7	8	9	R	H	E
LA	0	0	0	0	0	0	0	0	0	0	0	1
Cin	0	0	0	0	0	1	0	0	x	1	3	0

Los Angeles	IP	H	R	ER	BB	K
Belcher (L)	8	3	1	0	1	7

Cincinnati	IP	H	R	ER	BB	K
Browning (W)	9	0	0	0	0	7

Time—1:51; Att.—16,591

Reds teammates mobbed Browning after his dominating performance.

Orel Surgery

Sitting in the broadcast booth at Dodger Stadium, Don Drysdale was slowly watching his name being expunged from the record books, inning by inning, pitch by pitch.

Twenty years earlier, in what became known as "The Year of the Pitcher," when Bob Gibson had thrown 13 shutouts and had an earned run average of 1.12—the lowest in 54 years—and Dennis McLain had been baseball's first 30-game winner since Dizzy Dean in 1934, Drysdale had set an all-time record by pitching 58⅔ consecutive scoreless innings.

Now Big D, a broadcaster for the Dodgers, was watching another Dodgers right-hander, Orel Hershiser, take dead aim at a record some thought might never be broken.

Hershiser had been a Dodger since 1983 and had quickly become a mainstay of their pitching staff. When he won 19 games and lost only 3 in his second full season, Hershiser took his place alongside other outstanding Dodgers right-handers through the years: Dazzy Vance, Whitlow Wyatt, Don Newcombe, Carl Erskine, Don Sutton, Burleigh Grimes, and Drysdale. He picked up the nickname "Bulldog" from his manager Tommy Lasorda in admiration for Hershiser's feistiness and dogged competitiveness on the mound.

The 1988 season was Hershiser's best. He would tie for the National League lead in wins and complete games, and lead the league in shutouts and innings pitched. When he took the mound in San Diego's Jack Murphy Stadium on the night of September 28, in what would be his final start of the regular season, Hershiser had already won 23 games and lost only 8, and the Dodgers had clinched the National League West championship.

The game, however, meant more than wins and losses, for Hershiser was in the midst of a scoreless innings streak that threatened Drysdale's hallowed record.

The streak started on August 30 in Montreal when Hershiser shut down the Expos in the final four innings of a 4–2 win. In his next start in Atlanta on September 5, he shut out the Braves, 3–0. Five days later he blanked the Reds, 5–0. Then he shut out the Braves again, 1–0, and the Astros, 1–0, and the Giants, 3–0, on September 23 for his fifth straight shutout. (The Dodgers didn't score a lot of runs in those days and, in fact, scored only 13 during Hershiser's five consecutive shutouts.)

The shutout in Candlestick Park pushed Hershiser's scoreless streak to 49⅓ innings, leaving him 9⅔ innings behind Drysdale as he took the mound against the Padres. If he pitched another shutout, he would still need two more outs to catch Big D, so the plan was for him to pitch in relief in the final days of the season, but only to get the two outs to tie the record.

"Here's a great guy," Hershiser said of Drysdale, "a Hall of Famer, a Dodger. Why not just be tied together?"

Against the Padres, Hershiser continued his masterful roll. The Padres put a runner on in the first inning and another in the fourth, but failed to score. When Hershiser put the side down in order in the fifth and sixth, he was closing in on the record. In the seventh, Marvell Wynne singled with one out, but was stranded, and in the eighth, Robby Alomar singled with two outs (only the fourth hit off Hershiser) and quickly was picked off first base.

Now it was the ninth inning. Mike Flannery hit back to the box. One out. Tony Gwynn, the hit machine, grounded to second baseman Steve Sax. Two outs. Carmelo Martinez grounded to third baseman Jeff Hamilton. Inning over.

Because official baseball records do not recognize fractions of innings in pitchers' streaks, technically Hershiser had tied Drysdale's record at 58 consecutive scoreless innings. But that wasn't good enough for Hershiser. If he was to tie Drysdale, he wanted it to be an exact tie—58⅔ innings.

Unfortunately—or perhaps fortunately in this case—the Dodgers' offensive impotence continued against the Padres, and they too had not scored through nine innings. So the game went into the tenth, and Hershiser had his chance to catch Drysdale.

In the tenth Hershiser had to escape a jam of his own making when he struck out Marvell Wynne on a pitch in the dirt that eluded catcher Mike Scioscia. Wynne reached first base safely, was sacrificed to second, and moved to third on an infield out. Garry Templeton was walked intentionally, but Hershiser retired Keith Moreland on a fly ball to right. Hershiser had completed his night's work with 10 scoreless innings and passed Drysdale for the record.

After the game, which the Padres won 2–1 in 16 innings, Drysdale interviewed the man who had broken his record. When he heard that Hershiser was hoping to merely share the record with him, Drysdale said, "If I'd known that, I'd have kicked you in the rear and told you to get your buns out there and go for it."

Although it didn't count in the official records, Hershiser continued his streak in the postseason, when he pitched eight scoreless innings against the Mets in Game 1 of the National League Championship Series. The Mets then rallied for three runs in the ninth, after Hershiser had pitched 67 consecutive scoreless innings.

Hershiser shut out the Mets in Game 7 of the NLCS to advance the Dodgers to the World Series. And he pitched another shutout in Game 2 of the World Series against Oakland.

Officially, Hershiser's streak ended at 59 innings when he gave up a run to the Reds in the first inning of his first start in 1989.

> Hershiser had completed his night's work with 10 scoreless innings and passed Drysdale for the record.

Officially, Hershiser's streak ended six months after the 1988 World Series when he gave up a run in the first inning of his first start of 1989.

CHAPTER 29

Behind their white-hot ace and World Series MVP, the underdog Dodgers stunned the explosive A's in five games.

Hershiser commendably notched a 10-inning shutout performance to break Drysdale's record, then—though not applicable to regular-season records—continued the scoreless streak into the postseason.

A Divine Effort

Every pitcher who has thrown a perfect game had some help. Certainly from his teammates in the field, making often-spectacular plays. And the offense is key, too, of course, because without runs you can't be perfect. But Dennis Martinez can point to a little extra help on his way to his 1991 perfect game.

The Expos team bus left for Dodger Stadium at 10:30 A.M. for this Sunday matinee game, but Martinez had planned to attend mass at that time. He decided to go to church first, then the ballpark. The first thing he saw as he walked out of church was a cab, so he was at the ballpark by noon to warm up.

"Maybe if I don't go to church, I would be out in the first inning," he said. "Who knows? To me, that was the key point to the day."

Just arriving at any ballpark to play was a bit of a miracle for Martinez. He had to beat back and shoulder problems in the early eighties, and he defeated alcoholism that had threatened to end his career. He battled back through the minors and, by 1991, was one of the top pitchers in the NL. He entered the game leading the league with a 2.05 ERA (and would go on to win the league ERA title), and he was in the fifth of what would become ten straight seasons with 10-plus wins.

Matching Martinez pitch for pitch that afternoon was the Dodgers' Mike Morgan, as both pitchers were perfect through five innings. Morgan's own fly ball in the seventh, in fact, was the first ball hit to the outfield by the Dodgers against Martinez.

Expos center fielder Marquis Grissom had a perfect seat to watch Martinez at work. "He just made the right pitch every time. He had a good fastball, but it wasn't overpowering. He threw so many perfect pitches, right on the black. It was a beautiful thing to watch."

"We might have played 20 innings against him and never gotten a hit," said Dodgers catcher Mike Scioscia.

In the top of the seventh, with Martinez on third via an error, Larry Walker took a two-out, 2–2 pitch for ball three. Morgan (and later, Dodgers manager Tommy Lasorda) was steamed about the call. Walker took advantage, whacking the full-count pitch for a triple. He then scored when Alfredo Griffin made an error on Ron Hassey's grounder.

> "Maybe if I don't go to church, I would be out in the first inning. Who knows? To me, that was the key point to the day."
> —Dennis Martinez

As Martinez continued to nail Dodgers hitters, Expos catcher Hassey kept him pumped up. "He would catch the ball and point with his mitt, and go 'Yeah, yeah!' He was really psyching me up out there," said Martinez. "The intensity was really something."

The intensity ramped up thousands of miles to the south as well. Martinez was a huge hero in his native Nicaragua. Normally, his games were reported pitch-by-pitch via radio to local fans. But as this game went on, state television cut in to show the game live.

Scioscia led off the ninth by flying out to Ivan Calderon in right. Stan Javier struck out. That brought up Chris Gwynn. The Dodger Stadium crowd of more than forty-five thousand was already on its feet, showing by their cheers that they wanted to see a perfect game more than a Dodgers victory. Gwynn whacked a long fly to center and the huge crowd held its breath.

"That ball and the one in 1995 [that Grissom caught to close out the Braves' World Series championship] hung in the air longer than any ball I've ever seen," said Grissom. "I'm just telling the ball, 'C'mon down, c'mon down . . .' It was a happy moment for me, being a part of history, and also for our teammate who went out there and was an artist."

Following the celebration on the field, Martinez got a poignant reminder of just how far he had come to reach this amazing day. As the champagne flowed, he was careful not to drink any. "Remember, I told the guys, I don't drink. But that doesn't mean I can't celebrate!"

The inspirational nature of Martinez' day, one that started in church and ended in baseball heaven, continues to this day. It was first felt a month later when he returned to Nicaragua and was paraded through the streets. It had been a tough few years for the nation, and Martinez enjoyed giving them a release and a reason to cheer. Martinez's inspiration continues, as his work to aid his people goes on.

"I think there was a purpose to that game," he told *The Sporting News*. "This time more than any time, the people needed me to help them get back on track physically, spiritually, mentally. It's impossible to fill every heart, but I do what I can."

He did more than most can on that sunny day in L.A.

Martinez is thankful that he decided to take time out for a church service before heading out to Dodger Stadium on his greatest day as a pitcher.

DENNIS MARTINEZ'S PERFECT GAME
JULY 28, 1991

Montreal	AB	R	H	RBI
DeShields, 2b	3	0	1	0
Grissom, cf	4	0	0	0
Da. Martinez, rf	4	1	0	0
Calderon, lf	3	0	0	0
Wallach, 3b	4	0	0	0
Walker, 1b	4	1	1	1
Hassey, c	3	0	1	0
Owen, ss	3	0	0	0
De. Martinez, p	3	0	1	0
Totals	**31**	**2**	**4**	**1**

Los Angeles	AB	R	H	RBI
Butler, cf	3	0	0	0
Samuel, 2b	3	0	0	0
Murray, 1b	3	0	0	0
Strawberry, rf	3	0	0	0
Daniels, lf	3	0	0	0
Harris, 3b	3	0	0	0
Scioscia, c	3	0	0	0
Griffin, ss	2	0	0	0
Javier, ph	1	0	0	0
Morgan, p	2	0	0	0
Gwynn, ph	1	0	0	0
Totals	**27**	**0**	**0**	**0**

	1	2	3	4	5	6	7	8	9	R	H	E
Mon	0	0	0	0	0	0	2	0	0	2	4	0
LA	0	0	0	0	0	0	0	0	0	0	0	2

Montreal	IP	H	R	ER	BB	K
De. Martinez (W)	9	0	0	0	0	5

Los Angeles	IP	H	R	ER	BB	K
Morgan (L)	9	4	2	0	1	5

Time—2:14; Att.—45,560

Two Perfect

By backstopping Dennis Martinez in L.A., Ron Hassey made his own mark in the record books, becoming the first (and still only) catcher for two perfect games (he also caught Len Barker's). Number two was, for Hassey, more memorable.

"In about the seventh or eighth, I went to [pitching coach] Larry Bearnarth and told him we had a no-hitter in the bag. You don't want superstition to bite you in the ass, but this time around I was going to have a good time. In the ninth I told Larry, 'Watch this, it's going to be great.'

"It was really fun."

After having been admittedly oblivious to Barker's perfection, Hassey got a unique chance to go for two, and he made the most of it.

Living Out a Dream

In 1989, his rookie season, left-hander Jim Abbott won 12 games for the California Angels. It was remarkable. No, it was miraculous.

Abbott made it to the big leagues having never pitched a game in the minor leagues. That was the remarkable part. The miraculous part was that he did it without a right hand.

Jim was born with just a stump above the wrist at the end of his right arm. But he grew up with a love for sports and a desire to participate in the games kids play despite his disability, which he never let deter him. His story is one of courage and perseverance in the face of adversity. There was never any self-pity, and his parents never pampered him.

"I have never felt slighted," he once said. "As a kid I was pretty coordinated, and growing up, I loved sports. I learned to play baseball like most kids, playing catch with my dad in the front yard. The only difference was that we had to come up with a method to throw and catch with the same hand. What we came up with is basically what I continued to do my whole life. I used to practice by pretending to be my favorite pitchers. I'd throw a ball against a brick wall on the side of our house, switching the glove off and on, moving closer to the wall, forcing myself to get that glove on faster and faster.

"Sports were my way of gaining acceptance. I guess somewhere deep inside I was thinking if I was good enough on the field then maybe the kids would not think of me as being different. I wanted the attention that comes with being successful, but I was reluctant to draw attention to my disability. I didn't want to be defined by a disability. Focus on my pitching, not my hand."

At 11, Jim joined a Little League team and pitched a no-hitter in his first game. In high school, he was the quarterback on a football team that reached the Michigan state championship. In baseball, he pitched and batted .427 in his senior year with seven home runs and 31 RBIs.

At the University of Michigan, Abbott won 26 of the 34 games he pitched and was named to Team USA, which won a silver medal in the 1987 Pan American Games. Jim was named winner of the Sullivan Award, given annually by the Amateur Athletic Union to the country's outstanding amateur athlete.

In the 1988 Olympics, he pitched the United States to the gold medal by beating Japan in the championship game.

There was once a one-armed outfielder in the major leagues. His name was Pete Gray and he was a member of the St. Louis Browns in 1945, but while his courage was unquestioned and his ability to advance to the highest level of professional baseball was admirable, his playing career was undistinguished. He played in 77 games and batted .218.

Jim Abbott was not a great major league pitcher, never an All-Star, but he had a productive 10-year career, the winner of 87 games. In 1991, he won 18 games for the Angels, fourth most in the American League, and was fourth in earned run average, third in voting for the Cy Young Award. And on the afternoon of September 4, 1993, he achieved what all pitchers aspire to, and he did it on baseball's biggest stage: Yankee Stadium.

Abbott had been traded to the Yankees by the Angels on December 6, 1992. When he took the Yankee Stadium mound against the Cleveland Indians on that beautiful early September Saturday afternoon, he had won 9 games for the Yankees and lost 11, after losing five of his first six decisions.

> Earlier that season, on May 29 against the White Sox, he had lost a no-hitter with one out in the eighth inning. This time, when he retired the Indians in the eighth, he still had not allowed a hit.

Earlier that season, on May 29 against the White Sox, he had lost a no-hitter with one out in the eighth inning. This time, when he retired the Indians in the eighth, he still had not allowed a hit.

The Yankees had scored three runs in the third, another in the fifth, and went to the top of the ninth leading 4–0, the 27,125 fans in the stadium anxiously hoping to witness the first Yankee Stadium no-hitter since Dave Righetti's exactly 10 years and two months earlier.

When he put the Indians down in the ninth—he retired 11 of the last 12 batters, 14 of the last 16—Jim Abbott had pitched the 10th no-hitter in Yankees history.

When the final out was recorded, Abbott stood on the mound, arms raised in triumph. Photographers captured the pose. His glove is on his left hand. At the end of his upraised right arm is the stump above the wrist.

Nobody noticed.

Abbott acknowledges the cheers after holding Cleveland hitless on September 4, 1993.

JIM ABBOTT'S NO-HITTER
SEPTEMBER 4, 1993

Cleveland	AB	R	H	RBI
Lofton, cf	3	0	0	0
Fermin, ss	4	0	0	0
Baerga, 2b	4	0	0	0
Belle, lf	3	0	0	0
Milligan, 1b	1	0	0	0
Ramirez, dh	3	0	0	0
Maldonado, rf	3	0	0	0
Thome, 3b	2	0	0	0
Ortiz, c	1	0	0	0
Alomar, ph c	1	0	0	0
Milacki, p	0	0	0	0
Wertz, p	0	0	0	0
Totals	**25**	**0**	**0**	**0**

New York	AB	R	H	RBI
Boggs, 3b	4	1	1	0
James, lf	4	1	2	1
G. Williams, lf	0	0	0	0
Mattingly, 1b	3	0	1	0
Tartabull, dh	4	0	1	0
O'Neill, rf	4	0	0	0
B. Williams, cf	3	0	1	0
Nokes, c	4	0	1	0
Gallego, 2b	3	1	0	0
Valerde, ss	3	1	1	1
Abbott, p	0	0	0	0
Totals	**32**	**4**	**8**	**2**

	1	2	3	4	5	6	7	8	9		R	H	E
Cle	0	0	0	0	0	0	2	0	0		0	0	2
NYY	0	0	3	0	1	0	0	0	x		4	8	0

Cleveland	IP	H	R	ER	BB	K
Milacki (L)	5.1	6	4	2	3	2
Wertz	2.2	2	0	0	0	2

New York	IP	H	R	ER	BB	K
Abbott (W)	9	0	0	0	5	3

Time—2:33; Att.—27,125

Abbott's entry into the pantheon of unhittables is one of the more remarkable and inspirational stories in sports.

Mr. Rogers' Neighborhood

Though it didn't matter much to the Angels on July 28, 1994, Kenny Rogers was never supposed to be a major league pitcher. He was figuring on strawberry fields forever in his native Florida, when baseball lightning struck in the form of scout Joe Marchese. The Rangers' bird-dog was watching one of Rogers' high school teammates when he saw something in the 130-pound left-handed shortstop that made him take a second look. Marchese thought he saw a pitcher in that scrawny body, and darned if he wasn't right.

Of course, it took Rogers seven years to prove the scout right; Rogers even had to be taught how to pitch from a stretch position. But the former future strawberry picker made it to the majors in 1989. By the day of his perfect game in 1994 he had become a solid, if not spectacular, big league pitcher.

On July 28 of that year, however, Rogers was all that and more.

Rogers was 10–6 for the division-leading Rangers at that point in what would soon be a strike-shortened season. It was a night game against the California Angels in the brand-new Ballpark in Arlington, and more than forty-six thousand fans filled the place. Rogers remembers one fan in particular who watched him carefully during warm-ups. The fan was nodding his head "yes" for a good pitch, shaking "no" for a bad one. "Went on like that for the whole warm-up session," Rogers remembers. "After it was done I threw the ball up to him, but it went over his head to someone else. I'm sure wherever he is out there, he's still a little irritated."

Leadoff hitter Chad Curtis looked at a close 3–2 pitch for the first out and it was on. Rogers' teammates gave him two runs to start with. Jose Canseco got his second homer of the game in the third and Ivan Rodriguez followed that with another. Chris James and Gary Redus lit Canseco's shoes on fire in the fifth, but the splashing water that put out the flames did nothing to cool off Rogers.

In the seventh Rogers went to three-ball counts on all three hitters, but induced three more outs. The crowd was really getting into it by that time. Center fielder Rusty Greer said later, "From the seventh on, every ball was a boo and every strike a cheer."

In the eighth Rogers struck out Bo Jackson (for the third time) on a change-up that was "waaaay off the plate. I'd never had a guy swing at a pitch that far outside."

For the ninth the fans were all on their feet, but Rogers' eye was on the prize. "I never had one negative thought all game. And that's a rare thing."

Water on the Side

Players love superstitions. They're as much a part of baseball as sunflower seeds. During Kenny Rogers' perfect game, he had a little help with one unusual ritual.

"An assistant trainer gave me a cup of water after every inning. But then in the seventh, I sat down and he didn't show up. I knew I had the no-hitter going at that point, but for some reason, he hadn't brought it after a few minutes. I had been lining them up under the bench, some of them still half full, and I was looking for him. And I couldn't ask him, 'cause that would mess it up. Finally he did and I gave him a little look. He was right on time after that.

"After the game, I did an interview on the bench and looked down there and saw the eight water cups, all still lined up in a row."

> "When I left my feet, I knew I was going to catch it. It was just a matter of hanging on."
> —Rangers center fielder Rusty Greer

Halos second baseman Rex Hudler nearly gave everyone a big dose of negativity leading off the final inning. After whacking what he called a "frozen rope liner," Hudler took off running. In short center, so did Rusty Greer. Only a rookie, he was suddenly in position to save the day. "When I left my feet, I knew I was going to catch it. It was just a matter of hanging on," he said afterward. Hang on he did, making the greatest ninth-inning, perfect-game-saving catch in history.

"I never thought he was going to get it," Rogers said. "I thought it was going to drop." It did, but in the safety of Greer's glove. Following another out, Greer enjoyed a bonus thrill—catching a fly ball from Gary DiSarcina that was good for out number 27. The kid from the strawberry fields was in baseball history forever, and sometimes he just can't believe it.

"I can sit here now in my 20th pro season [in 2001] and I just don't think you can comprehend how many things had to go just right to get me to pitch in the big leagues, let alone pitch a perfect game." Rogers' story is, well, perfect.

Rogers signaled to the crowd after recording the 26th out of his perfect game, then retired number 27 to gain membership into one of baseball's most exclusive fraternities.

KENNY ROGERS' PERFECT GAME
JULY 28, 1994

California	AB	R	H	RBI
Curtis, cf	3	0	0	0
Owen, 3b	3	0	0	0
Edmonds, lf	3	0	0	0
Davis, dh	3	0	0	0
Jackson, rf	3	0	0	0
Snow, 1b	3	0	0	0
Hudler, 2b	3	0	0	0
Turner, c	3	0	0	0
Discarnia, ss	3	0	0	0
Lorraine, p	0	0	0	0
Springer, p	0	0	0	0
Totals	**27**	**0**	**0**	**0**

Texas	AB	R	H	RBI
Davis, rf	4	0	0	0
Rodriguez, c	3	1	1	1
Canseco, dh	4	2	2	2
Clark, 1b	3	1	0	0
Gonzalez, lf	4	0	2	0
Palmer, 3b	4	0	1	1
Greer, cf	3	0	0	0
Lee, 2b	3	0	0	0
Beltre, ss	2	0	0	0
Rogers, p	0	0	0	0
Totals	**30**	**4**	**6**	**4**

	1	2	3	4	5	6	7	8	9	R	H	E
Cal	0	0	0	0	0	0	0	0	0	0	0	0
Tex	2	0	2	0	0	0	0	0	x	4	6	0

California	IP	H	R	ER	BB	K
Lorraine (L)	6.2	6	4	4	2	4
Springer	1.1	0	0	0	1	1

Texas	IP	H	R	ER	BB	K
Rogers (W)	9	0	0	0	0	8

Time—2:08; Att.—46,581

PART IV

Today

1995 to the Present

Phil Pepe's Top 20 Pitchers of All Time

1. Sandy Koufax
2. Walter Johnson
3. Bob Feller
4. Warren Spahn
5. Christy Mathewson
6. Bob Gibson
7. Tom Seaver
8. Steve Carlton
9. Grover Cleveland Alexander
10. Roger Clemens
11. Cy Young
12. Lefty Grove
13. Juan Marichal
14. Nolan Ryan
15. Randy Johnson
16. Whitey Ford
17. Pedro Martinez
18. Carl Hubbell
19. Robin Roberts
20. Ferguson Jenkins

James Buckley Jr.'s Top 20 Pitchers of All Time

1. Christy Mathewson
2. Walter Johnson
3. Sandy Koufax
4. Roger Clemens
5. Lefty Grove
6. Randy Johnson
7. Warren Spahn
8. Cy Young
9. Bob Gibson
10. Grover Cleveland Alexander
11. Bob Feller
12. Addie Joss
13. Greg Maddux
14. Tom Seaver
15. Steve Carlton
16. Satchel Paige
17. Ed Walsh
18. Juan Marichal
19. Nolan Ryan
20. Dennis Eckersley

Nearly Perfect

Baseball's magical lure is that each new game presents an opportunity to see something incredible. Whenever a superstar pitcher gets through the line-up a couple of times with seeming ease, fans watching at home and in the park all start to wonder, "Will this be the day?" as a hurler cruises untouched through five. But even superstars fall short and become members of the Nearly Perfect team.

The margin between perfection and just another great outing is razor-thin. To pitch a perfect game, a pitcher must step carefully along the razor's edge with nary a nick or cut. Only 16 men have reached the far end. Dozens more slip off, the most agonizing come late in their walk along that edge. That one final misstep is magnified by the difference between those who have completed the journey and those who have not. The pitcher who comes within one batter of perfection doesn't get his picture on the front page of a newspaper, the key to the city, or a place in the record books. In baseball, nearly perfect isn't good enough.

On June 3, 1995, Pedro Martinez, then 23 years old and with the Montreal Expos, became the second pitcher to take a perfecto into extra innings. Like Harvey Haddix (see Chapter 18), the captain of the Nearly Perfect team, Martinez is not included among the list of perfect game pitchers. Yet anyone who was there at San Diego's Jack Murphy Stadium saw a performance that was one for the books. Martinez stifled the Padres with a perfor-mance that foreshadowed his later domination of the American League with the Boston Red Sox.

Of the first 27 outs, 9 came on strikeouts, 8 on fly balls to the outfield, 2 on line drives caught in the infield, 4 on ground balls, and 4 on infield pop-ups. After nine scoreless innings, the Expos broke through for a 1–0 lead in the top of the tenth, giving Martinez a chance for the first extra-inning perfect game in baseball history.

Unfortunately, the 28th batter spoiled the fairy-tale ending. Bip Roberts broke up perfection by leading off the bottom of the tenth with a line-drive double that landed just inside the right-field foul line. The hit came on a 1–1 change-up that was Martinez's 96th pitch of the game. Three outs later, Martinez had a 1–0 victory, but under the amended rule, he receives no credit for a perfect game or a no-hitter. Joe Kerrigan, who was then the Montreal pitching coach and was later Martinez's coach and manager in Boston, was opposed to the amended rule on perfect games.

"For Pedro not to get credit for a perfect game is a shame," he told *Sports Illustrated*. "This belongs in the annals of baseball. You can't

So Close . . .

Few pitchers have ever blown a perfect game as tragically as Hooks Wiltse, a left-hander who won 139 games for the New York Giants between 1904 and 1914. Wiltse's most successful season was in 1908, when he won 23 games with seven shutouts. The southpaw's best performance that year was a no-hitter he pitched against the Philadelphia Phillies on July 4 in the first game of a doubleheader. Wiltse won the game, 1–0, in 10 innings, but it could have been a perfect game. With two outs in the bottom of the ninth, Wiltse was facing the opposing pitcher, George McQuillan, and with a two-strike count—plunk!—Wiltse hit McQuillan with a pitch. It was the only time a pitcher lost a perfect game by hitting the final batter.

Ouch.

Dick Bosman of the Cleveland Indians has nobody but himself to blame for blowing his perfect game opportunity. Bosman kept the world champion Oakland Athletics in check with a no-hitter on July 19, 1974, but was denied perfection by his own throwing error. Sal Bando hit a chopper back to the box and Bosman threw wildly to first base.

"It's a play I make a hundred times," said Bosman. "But that time I didn't."

> ## Like Harvey Haddix, the captain of the Nearly Perfect team, Martinez is not included among the list of perfect game pitchers.

pass this off as just another game, but that's how it will go down—as just another game."

To be sure, baseball fans appreciate great pitching performances for the remarkable achievements they are. It doesn't matter where they rank in the record book. On September 2, 2001, Mike Mussina of the New York Yankees was one strike away from being the fourth Yankee to hurl a perfecto. Thanks to his pinpoint control, the 32-year-old right-hander mowed down Red Sox with little fanfare, and in fact, with little help. He struck out 8 of the first 13 Boston batters. In the sixth inning, Shea

Martinez was a 23-year-old Montreal Expo when he came within inches of throwing the first extra-inning perfect game in history.

Mussina, having come within one strike of a perfect game once and taken two into the ninth inning, is a charter member of the snakebitten Nearly Perfect team.

Stieb, who finally got his no-hitter in 1990, flirted with perfection numerous times as one of the game's most dominant pitchers of the eighties.

Hillenbrand hit the first ball of the game to the outfield, flying out to Bernie Williams. Mike Lansing popped to Paul O'Neill (who was on the winning team in three perfect games), and Joe Oliver was the third out.

Mussina got through the seventh inning with no trouble, but the Yankees still hadn't scored a run. In the eighth, Mussina went to 3–2 on Manny Ramirez, but Manny popped to Derek Jeter. Dante Bichette flew to Williams, and Brian Daubach looked at strike three. Mussina knew he was close to achieving a perfect game and, superstitions be damned, had no problem admitting it.

"I thought about it every inning," he said.

Mussina is no stranger to near-perfect games. This marked the third time in his career that he had taken a bid for a perfect game into the eighth inning. He came within two outs of a perfect game in 1997, and within four outs in 1998, while pitching for the Baltimore Orioles.

The Yankees finally pushed a run across in the ninth inning. Now Mussina had his chance. He had a run, but did he have the stuff? With Fenway's fans oddly quiet, Troy O'Leary drove a hard grounder that seemed ticketed for right field. But first baseman Clay Bellinger dove full-out to his right, snared the ball, and flipped it to Mussina for the out.

"After Clay made that play," Mussina said afterward, "I thought that this might be the time that it happens."

Lou Merloni came up and became Mussina's 13th strikeout victim with little trouble. Now Mussina had retired the first 26 Boston Red Sox batters in order and was just one batter away, but that batter was Carl Everett, pinch hitting. Bing, bing, it was 0–2. Now Mussina was in very rare territory, one strike away. Everett took a ball high.

"You never think it's going to happen," manager Joe Torre said later, "until there are two out and two strikes. Then you feel like he's going to get it."

On the next pitch, Mussina left a ball a bit high and Everett swung. The ball flew on a looping line into left-center field and landed safely. A clean base hit. Perfect game over. Trot Nixon grounded out to follow and the game was over, too.

"Yeah, I was disappointed," Mussina said afterward. "That's the second time I've been to the ninth, and I didn't get it either time. So it's probably not meant to be."

Perhaps Mussina's next start will be the one. Hey, you never know.

Dave Stieb of the Toronto Blue Jays is an exalted member of the Nearly Perfect fraternity. On August 4, 1989, the 6'1", 195-pound right-hander was cruising through 8⅔ innings against the New York Yankees at Toronto's Skydome. He retired the first 26 batters to face him, 11 by strikeout. With two down in the ninth inning, Stieb's first two pitches to Roberto Kelly were called balls.

"I didn't do myself any favors by falling behind," said Stieb.

His 84th pitch of the game was a slider down and away. Kelly lined the ball sharply to left field for a double, shattering Stieb's bid for a no-hit, perfect game. When Steve Sax followed with a single, that ended the shutout, too, but the Jays and Stieb held on for a 2–1, two-hit victory. Winning is anticlimactic when the winning pitcher feels disappointed.

"Baseball can be a strange game," said Stieb, who seemed particularly jinxed during his 16-year career. "Sometimes, it's easier to pitch when you give up an early hit. It takes the pressure off."

If ever there was a hard-luck pitcher, it's Stieb. He nearly duplicated Johnny Vander Meer's feat of pitching consecutive no-hit games. Twice over a six-day period in September 1988, Stieb was one out away from a no-hitter when a bad hop and a bloop, respectively, shattered his potential gems. Stieb finally reached the Holy Grail, pitching that elusive no-hitter, in 1990.

"It's funny," Stieb wrote in his autobiography, *Tomorrow I'll Be Perfect*, "when I finally did get the no-hitter, I didn't have as good stuff as I did the other games. I guess that time it was just meant to be."

Stieb's nod to fate might be the very best way of all to explain why it must be heartbreaking to pitch the game of your dreams, only to be pinched by the 27th batter. On April 20, 1990, Brian Holman of the Seattle Mariners lost his bid for a perfect game with two outs in the ninth inning when Ken Phelps clubbed a pinch-hit home run over the right-field wall at the Oakland Coliseum. Moments before, there had been a brief delay as the pinch-hitter was announced and Phelps appeared in the on-deck circle. Holman's mind began to wander.

"I'm thinking to myself, 'You're one out away from the Hall of Fame.' I actually began to think, 'Will my glove or my jersey be on display in Cooperstown?' It was an out-of-body experience. The Oakland fans were cheering for me, and though I was a part of what was happening, I was watching it all take place from somewhere else."

He should have stayed where he was instead of taking that trip to nowhere. Holman threw 103 perfect pitches and one that missed by an inch. Phelps turned that inch into a 370-foot homer. One pitch, one home run: good-bye perfect game, no-hitter, and shutout.

Holman admitted that he didn't sleep at all the night after his near-perfecto.

"In the hotel room at 4:00 in the morning I realized I'd never get that close again. I put a pillow over my face and screamed."

Nothing is more bittersweet than a pitcher on the precipice of perfection who has to settle for a one-hitter. Milt Wilcox of the Detroit Tigers is still second-guessing a pitch he threw more than 20 years ago. On April 15, 1983, Wilcox was pitching superbly against the Chicago White Sox at Comiskey Park. He had retired all 26 batters to come to the plate and was one out away from a perfect game when Chicago pinch-hitter Jerry Hairston ripped a clean single through the box.

"It was the worst pitch I made all night," said Wilcox, who had doubled over on the mound, like a man sick to his stomach, after the spell was broken. "Pitch a perfect game and you go in the Hall of Fame. That's the only way I'd go there."

Mussina, Stieb, Wilcox, and Holman were one pitch away from Cooperstown and baseball immortality. If only they'd gotten one more out. If only . . .

Wilcox was just an out away, but had to settle for Nearly Perfect.

Members Only

Which of the following pitchers has never struck out 20 batters in a major league game?

    a) Steve Carlton
    b) Tom Cheney
    c) Roger Clemens
    d) Randy Johnson
    e) Kerry Wood

If you said b), the logical answer, your membership in the baseball trivia Hall of Fame has been revoked. The correct answer is a).

Steve Carlton holds the National League record for strikeouts by a left-hander with 19, but he never struck out 20 batters in a game. The four others did, including Tom Cheney. There is an asterisk attached, however.

On September 12, 1962, Cheney struck out 21 Orioles, a team that included Brooks Robinson and Boog Powell. But it took him 16 innings to do it. Clemens, twice, and Wood struck out 20 in nine innings. So did Randy Johnson, but the game went 11 (the Unit left after nine), and he also gets that infernal asterisk.

If we're talking asterisks, note that both of Clemens' 20-strikeout games came when he was pitching for the Red Sox, and Johnson twice struck out 19 in a game when he was a member of the Seattle Mariners, which means they did it in games in which there was a designated hitter, and didn't have the benefit of facing an opposing pitcher. The other high strikeout totals—Cheney's 21, Wood's 20, and Carlton's 19 came either in the National League or BDH—Before the Designated Hitter.

Not surprisingly, the list of high strikeout games is headed by some of the game's greatest strikeout pitchers—Clemens, Johnson (Randy and Walter), Nolan Ryan, Tom Seaver, Bob Gibson, Bob Feller. The one notable exception is Cheney, whose inclusion on the list looks like a typographical error.

In eight seasons with the Cardinals, Pirates, and Senators, Cheney won only 19 games, with a high of eight wins for Washington in 1963. In 1962, the year of his 21 Ks, he struck out 147 batters, a career high. He never struck out as many as 100 in any other year, and the only season he struck out more batters than innings pitched was his first, 1957, nine innings, 10 Ks.

Cheney had a great arm, and not much luck. Of his 19 career victories, eight were shutouts. But chronic arm problems curtailed his effectiveness and cut short his career. On the night he struck out 21 Orioles, he had a hellacious curveball, and who knows what else.

The Senators scored a run in the top of the sixteenth, and Cheney finished off the 2–1 victory by getting Dick Williams for the final out, his 21st strikeout.

Clemens, "the Rocket," was 23 years, eight months, and 25 days old when he faced the Seattle Mariners in Fenway Park on April 29, 1986, his third season with the Red Sox in a career that would extend more than 20 years, and in which he would win six Cy Young Awards, five strikeout championships, and record more than 4,000 Ks.

In his 20-K run against the Mariners, Clemens had 12 strikeouts swinging, eight looking, struck out the side in the first and again in the fourth and fifth (all three looking), struck out eight straight batters from the fourth to the sixth, struck out every Mariners starter—including Phil Bradley four times, had at least one strikeout in every inning, and finished up with two strikeouts in each of the last four innings. He pitched a three-hitter and won, 3–1.

A decade later, on September 18, 1996, Clemens pitched a five-hit shutout against the Tigers in Detroit and became the only pitcher in major league history to twice strike out 20 batters in a game. Again he struck out every opposing starter, and inflicted on Tigers shortstop Travis Fryman, baseball's "Golden Sombrero," four strikeouts.

In his 20-strikeout gem for the Diamondbacks against the Reds on May 8, 2001, Randy Johnson was removed from the game after nine innings with the score tied, 1–1. Johnson, whose career includes five Cy Young Awards, eight strikeout championships, and six seasons with more than 300 Ks—with a high of 364 in 1999—had allowed just three hits and, like Clemens' two gems, had struck out every starter in the Reds' lineup. Arizona won the game, 4–3, in 11 innings.

Some have made the case that Kerry Wood's 20-strikeout game for the Cubs against the Astros on May 6, 1998, was the most dominant pitching performance ever. In addition to the Ks (he struck out every Astro, including pinch-hitter Bill Spiers), Wood allowed only one hit, a debatable infield single by Ricky Gutierrez that could have been ruled an error.

At the time, Wood was only 20 years, 10 months, and 17 days old, and on his way to the National League Rookie of the Year award.

Because they are both Texans and hard throwers, Wood has been compared to Clemens, his pitching idol. Another comparison is this: in his first five years, Kerry Wood has struck out 1,065 batters; in his first five years, Roger Clemens struck out 985.

> A decade later, on September 18, 1996, Clemens pitched a five-hit shutout against the Tigers in Detroit and became the only pitcher in major league history to twice strike out 20 batters in a game.

Many experts list Wood's 20-K performance (at age 20) of 1998 among
the most dominating pitching performances of all time.

Clemens notched the second 20 strikeout game of his career on September 18, 1996 (left), exactly 10 seasons after fanning 20 Seattle Mariners on a memorable April evening at Fenway (above).

Perfect He Was

When he joined the Yankees in 1997, David Wells served notice that he would be a throwback not only to the Bronx Zoo days, but even farther back than that. Along with sporting numerous tattoos and dropping quote bombs like this one—"I'm just the kind of guy who is going to give the manager crap. Joe Torre knows that and he has to deal with it."—he also showed his love of Yankee tradition by buying an old cap of Babe Ruth's and proceeding to wear it (briefly) during a game. He also chose No. 33 in honor of Ruth's retired No. 3.

On May 17 Wells took his connections to his much-loved Yankees even further. He matched Don Larsen (like Wells, a graduate of Point Loma High in San Diego) by becoming the second Yankees pitcher ever to toss a perfect game. Like Larsen, too, Wells brought a sturdy if unremarkable record to the mound, and like Larsen, he brought a reputation that spoke of curfews missed and bars closed. In fact, in his 2002 autobiography, *Perfect I'm Not*, Wells says that he entered that May game against the Minnesota Twins with a bit of a hangover.

It was a gray day at Yankee Stadium, and a huge crowd (49,820) filled the place for Beanie Baby Day. A stuffed white bear with a red heart sewn in the chest was given out to kids 14 and under. (After the game, not surprisingly, enterprising New Yorkers had assembled at the exit gates offering tidy sums for the now-more-valuable bears.) Wells came into the game at 4–1, but with a 5.23 ERA and bouncing back from a third-inning pull in his previous start.

"Early on you had the feeling he had great stuff," said Yankees broadcaster Michael Kay. "But when you think of perfection, you don't think of David Wells."

Wells has always been a great control pitcher, often among league leaders in fewest walks allowed, but by being around the plate, he gives up perhaps more than his share of hits. But on this perfect day, the hits weren't coming. Wells struck out the side in the third, after the Yanks had given him his first run. In that inning, he went to the first of several three-ball counts on hitters, but always managed to work his way out.

As the innings wore on and Twins kept returning to the dugout, first the Yankees and then the fans started paying closer attention. "I didn't even know what was going on until the sixth inning," said Wells. "I knew I had a no-hitter, but didn't think about the perfect game. But then the fans started really getting into it."

> "Early on you had the feeling he had great stuff. But when you think of perfection, you don't think of David Wells."
> —Yankees broadcaster Michael Kay

On the radio, Kay and partner John Sterling were telling listeners to call their friends, that this was something special not to be missed.

With a comfortable 4–0 lead by the seventh, Wells battled future Hall of Famer Paul Molitor to a 3–1 count before inducing a ground-ball out. "Once he got Molly out," said Torre after the game, "he was going to pitch a perfect game. That's being tested by a big-time hitter."

"That was probably one of my best pitches of the game," Wells said in the locker room.

Wells was certainly aware of what was up, and his teammates were avoiding him studiously. All except fellow pitcher David Cone, who calmed down the nervous pitcher by telling him that "it was time to break out the knuckleball."

In the eighth, everyone got a little nervous when Ron Coomer hit a smash up the middle. Chuck Knoblauch moved quickly to his right, corralled the ball, and got Coomer at first. After that inning, Cone kept up the calming chatter. "Come on, man," he told Wells. "You're not showing me anything!"

As the ninth began it was nearly pandemonium, with every fan on their feet. Wells, of course, noticed. "The fans were going crazy, which was great, but I kind of wanted them to calm down because they were making me nervous. By the end I could barely grip the ball, my hand was shaking so much."

Fans in the Bronx were not the only ones. For the first time, millions around the country could watch the action live, as ESPN broke into regular coverage to telecast the final inning. Thanks to cable, the universe of people who can say they *saw* a perfect game expanded dramatically.

While they all watched Wells, "The only thing I saw was Jorge [Posada]'s glove," said Wells. "Thank goodness for tunnel vision." Two quick outs brought the crescendo to a fever pitch, which erupted even louder when Pat Meares' lazy fly ball landed in Paul O'Neill's mitt. Wells watched it all the way and leaped into the air as the out was recorded . . . and more Yankees history was made.

After the game, Wells got a call from his fellow Point Loma alum, Don Larsen. Yogi Berra said it took him back to that day in 1956. Comedian Billy Crystal came into the locker room with a now-famous quote, "I got here late . . . what happened?" Mayor Rudy Giuliani gave Wells the key to the city and a "day" in New York. The accolades poured in nearly as thickly as the celebratory beverages would for several days.

David Wells will never be Babe Ruth, and he wasn't even a Yankee for much longer. But for one day, the supposedly "imperfect" man was perfect, and a perfect addition to a century of Yankees lore.

Wells watched the final out of his perfect game disappear into right fielder
Paul O'Neill's glove, and the party was about to begin.

DAVID WELLS' PERFECT GAME
MAY 17, 1998

Minnesota	AB	R	H	RBI
Lawton, cf	3	0	0	0
Gates, 2b	3	0	0	0
Molitor, dh	3	0	0	0
Cordova, lf	3	0	0	0
Coomer, 1b	3	0	0	0
Ochoa, rf	3	0	0	0
Shave, 3b	3	0	0	0
Valentin, c	3	0	0	0
Meares, ss	3	0	0	0
Hawkins, p	0	0	0	0
Naulty, p	0	0	0	0
Swindell, p	0	0	0	0
Totals	**27**	**0**	**0**	**0**

New York	AB	R	H	RBI
Knoblauch, 2b	4	0	0	0
Jeter, ss	3	0	1	0
O'Neill, rf	4	0	0	0
Martinez, 1b	4	0	0	0
Williams, cf	3	3	3	1
Strawberry, dh	3	1	1	1
Curtis, lf	3	0	1	1
Posada, c	3	0	0	0
Brosius, 3b	3	0	0	0
Wells, p	0	0	0	0
Totals	**30**	**4**	**6**	**3**

	1	2	3	4	5	6	7	8	9	R	H	E
Min	0	0	0	0	0	0	0	0	0	0	0	0
NYY	0	1	0	1	0	0	2	0	x	4	6	0

Minnesota	IP	H	R	ER	BB	K
Hawkins (L)	7	6	4	4	0	5
Naulty	0.1	0	0	0	1	0
Swindell	0.2	0	0	0	0	1

New York	IP	H	R	ER	BB	K
Wells (W)	9	0	0	0	0	11

Time—2:40; Att.—49,820

Déjà Vu All Over Again

So many things have to go just right to make a perfect game. Every pitch must be in just the right spot, every batted ball hit toward a fielder, every umpire's call just what is needed, and every defensive play handled flawlessly. In a game that can begin anew with each pitch, there are hundreds of chances for something to go wrong. The perfect game, along with being a reflection of a pitcher reaching the ultimate unhittable goal, is a celebration of synchronicity.

On July 18, 1999, coincidence, synchronicity, and good timing came together as never before or since. Not only did David Cone pitch the 14th and final perfect game of the 20th century, he did it with so many parallels and links to the past that it was beyond uncanny—it was baseball.

In 1956, Don Larsen had pitched the Yankees' first perfect game, right there in Yankee Stadium in the World Series. His catcher was Yogi Berra. In 1999, Cone took the mound literally in Larsen's footsteps. The older pitcher had thrown out the first ball on Yogi Berra Day. . . . Berra had caught it and then handed the mitt to Joe Girardi, Cone's backstop. Berra had returned after a too-long absence from Yankeeland, in protest of previous poor treatment at the hands of owner George Steinbrenner. But all was forgiven and forty-one thousand fans came out on a sunny Sunday afternoon to share the love with Yogi. His uniform No. 8 (presciently, as we will see) was painted in front of each dugout.

Watching from the dugout was Yankees manager Joe Torre, celebrating his 59th birthday—and what a present he would get. Torre had been in the same spot the year before for David Wells' perfect game, and had been in the stands as a teenager for Larsen's.

The connections were eerie, and nearly as baffling as the pitches Cone was soon flinging past the hapless Montreal Expos.

"Cone had unbelievable stuff," remembers Yankees broadcaster Michael Kay. "But his breaking ball was breaking so much, they would have walked if they'd just taken pitches. But being a young team, the Expos were swinging at everything."

Manager Felipe Alou had had a premonition about that. "As I finished writing out the lineup card," he said afterward, "I realized that not one of the nine players had ever faced Cone before." Trotting out a team of first-timers to face a veteran like Cone was like letting the ballboys receive serve against Pete Sampras.

> "As I finished writing out the lineup card, I realized that not one of the nine players had ever faced Cone before."
> —Expos manager Felipe Alou

(A trivial side note with yet another Larsen connection: as part of the interleague baseball revolution of 1997, this was the first perfect game pitched by one league against the other since Larsen's Series gem.)

Cone survived an early defensive scare when Paul O'Neill had to dive to snag a looper hit by Terry Jones. The pitcher and his mates then waited out a 33-minute rain delay in the third inning caused by a passing thunderstorm. "It was so humid," Cone said, "I had no problem staying loose."

With a 5–0 lead courtesy of homers by Ricky Ledee and Derek Jeter, Cone was able to go after every hitter. By the fifth, Kay and partner John Sterling were not only well aware of what was transpiring, they were rooting it on.

"Anyone who tells me that I can change something about the game by talking about it on the air, then I want to get paid a lot more money," Sterling laughs. "We talked about Cone's game very early on."

The fans in the stands were aware of the situation, too. "Our section was definitely in tune to the perfect game by the fourth inning," says Yankees fan and writer David Fischer, who watched from his seat behind home plate. "On Yogi Berra Day, with Larsen there, and remembering what Wells had done . . . we were counting down the outs early."

Larsen nearly wasn't there for the end. *Sports Illustrated* reported after the game that he had gotten up to leave but had been called back when reminded that Cone was then working toward matching the old pitcher's perfection.

Also counting outs was Montreal shortstop Orlando Cabrera. "In the sixth, we realized what he was doing. I did the math and realized that if he kept doing what he was doing, I'd be the last batter."

Another interested party had some perspective to lend to the situation, and it didn't look good for his team. Expos coach Tommy Harper had been on the Montreal staff back in 1991 when Dennis Martinez threw his perfect game. "This one was like Dennis'," Harper said. "Cone had everything working. He was hitting all his spots and never with the same arm angle."

In the eighth, things were momentarily scary for Cone and the Yankees fans. Jose Vidro smacked a hard grounder up the middle. Moving quickly to get to it was second baseman Chuck Knoblauch. Now even on a routine play, Knoblauch's arm was suspect, especially so at that time as he was in the midst of one of his occasional Steve Sax–like throwing slumps. But he fired unerringly to first after snatching up the ball and got Vidro by a step.

On a day filled with déjà vu, several observers pointed out that Knoblauch had done almost the exact same thing in the exact same spot for Wells 14 months earlier.

There was an eerie feeling of familiarity at Yankee Stadium during Cone's perfect game in 1999, thrown on the day of a tribute to Yogi Berra.

The ninth was played at the bottom of a bowl of noise. All the fans in the place were on their feet cheering every move Cone made. "My heart was pounding through my uniform," Cone said later. "I've wondered if I'd ever get a chance again. Going into the later innings, that was running through my mind, about how many times I'd been close and how this might be the last chance I get."

Chris Widger was an easy K for out number one. Pinch-hitter Ryan McGuire then smacked a 2–2 pitch on a low line toward Ledee in left. "As we were talking during the game," a relieved Ledee said some time later, "I told everyone that if a ball is hit to me after about the seventh, it might be trouble with the sun. It was an easy play I made hard because I couldn't see the ball."

Ledee charged the sinking liner blindly. From third, Scott Brosius ran out to coach his teammate toward the ball. "Go right, go right . . . put the glove down." Whether coaxed in by Brosius or pushed in by helpful Yankees ghosts, the ball smacked into Ledee's glove, surprising him as much as anyone. Two outs, one more to go for perfection.

As predicted, Cabrera represented out number 27. "I thought, 'This is the biggest at-bat of my career. If I break up this perfect game or the no-hitter, it would be awesome to do it in New York. Of course, I may not get out alive if I did.' I went to hit and told Girardi, 'Throw whatever you want, I'm here to swing.' "

On the third pitch, Cabrera did just that. He got under it, though, and lofted a short pop foul down the third-base line. Brosius rolled in, waving his arms like a traffic cop. "I remember looking at the film later," he said. "And I was worried that Girardi might run into me. But he was already at the mound hugging Coney. I was all alone out there."

The ball dropped into Brosius' glove and the place just erupted. The sound was deafening and would go on for some minutes. Girardi was indeed hugging Cone, who had dropped to his knees, his hands clasped to his head in disbelief. Girardi hugged him and then pulled him to the ground on top of him.

"I have been under a lot of piles," said the ever-protective catcher. "I didn't want him to be at the bottom."

After a few minutes of dog piling and backslapping, a few Yankees roughly lifted Cone to their shoulders. Waving his cap to the crowd, Cone rode off in triumph.

Larsen watched, applauding. Berra was smiling and cheering.

They were in the most unique positions of anyone in the park. Some others there might have witnessed games. But they had lived it. And now through Cone's magic, they lived it again.

Perfect, just perfect.

DAVID CONE'S PERFECT GAME
JULY 18, 1999

Montreal	AB	R	H	RBI
W. Guerrero, dh	3	0	0	0
Jones, cf	2	0	0	0
Mouton, cf	1	0	0	0
White, lf	3	0	0	0
V. Guerrero, rf	3	0	0	0
Vidro, 2b	3	0	0	0
Fullmer, 1b	3	0	0	0
Widger, c	3	0	0	0
Andrews, 3b	2	0	0	0
McGuire, ph	1	0	0	0
Cabrera, ss	3	0	0	0
Vazquez, p	0	0	0	0
Ayala, p	0	0	0	0
Totals	**27**	**0**	**0**	**0**

New York	AB	R	H	RBI
Knoblauch, 2b	2	1	1	0
Jeter, ss	4	1	1	2
O'Neill, rf	4	1	1	0
Williams, cf	4	0	1	1
Martinez, 1b	4	0	1	0
Davis, dh	3	1	1	0
Ledee, lf	4	1	1	2
Brosius, 3b	2	1	0	0
Girardi, c	3	0	1	1
Cone, p	0	0	0	0
Totals	**30**	**6**	**8**	**6**

	1	2	3	4	5	6	7	8	9		R	H	E
Mon	0	0	0	0	0	0	0	0	0		0	0	0
NYY	0	5	0	0	0	0	0	1	x		6	8	0

Montreal	IP	H	R	ER	BB	K
Vazquez (L)	7	7	6	6	2	3
Ayala	1	0	0	0	0	0

New York	IP	H	R	ER	BB	K
Cone (W)	9	0	0	0	0	10

Time—2:16; Att.—41,930

Cone receives a congratulatory handshake from Larsen, who was one of the many Yankee greats in attendance for the Berra tribute.

CHAPTER 36

Aging Gracefully

Creeaakkk!

That sound you hear is not Randy Johnson's surgically repaired right knee. It's not the aging back of the 40-year-old pitcher. It's not the sound most of us 40-year-olds make when we try to do something as physical as pitch a baseball.

No, that creak is the sound made by critics sneaking out the door. The same critics who said that Johnson, after an injury-plagued 2003, was on the downhill slope of his Hall of Fame career. They had nothing to say when he wrapped up the 17th perfect game in baseball history—and the first pitched by someone with four decades of life under his belt. Fanning 13, the second most ever in a perfect game, Johnson shut down the Atlanta Braves 2–0 and cemented his already solid place as one of the top left-handed pitchers the game has ever seen.

The mumbling about Johnson being over the hill were loud in 2003, when he pitched in only a handful of games due to two stints on the DL. They continued as he started 2004 with a un-RJ-like 4–4 record into the May 18 start. Of course, a "bad" beginning to a season for Johnson would be a career year for most pitchers. Though he had lost the four games heading into his perfecto, he led the league in Ks per nine innings with more than 11, and opponents were hitting a paltry .156 against him, the lowest mark in either league.

Of course, it's not like he came out of nowhere to reach perfection. In 2002 he became the second player ever to have won five Cy Youngs (behind Roger Clemens' six), the second with four in a row (following Greg Maddux's 1992–1995 streak), and bested even the great Sandy Koufax with four straight seasons topping 300 strikeouts. He also won his first pitching triple crown that year. Those feats of course all followed his magical 2001 season, when he added a World Series ring and a co-MVP trophy to his Cy Young Award (a season that also included his career-best 372 Ks). And his stunning run with the Diamondbacks came after an awesome career with Seattle, capped by his 20–4, 2.28 season in 1997.

Yet Arizona manager Bob Brenly, after watching his ace mow down the Braves, said, "Everything he's done up to this point pales in comparison." Johnson now has the tiny class of perfect-game pitchers with which to compare himself.

It was a hot and steamy Atlanta night when Johnson, at the aforementioned 4–4, took the mound against the Braves. "With the humidity, you get loose

Two for the Mike

A fun sidelight to the Randy Johnson story, especially in light of the other perfect games highlighted in this book, is that Johnson's featured another interesting first. Arizona play-by-play man Thom Brenneman joined his dad Marty as the only father-and-son duo to each call a perfect game. Marty was on the scene and on the air for Tom Browning's gem in 1988. The two spoke after the game and were able to share feelings that few others, and certainly no other family members, have shared.

pretty quick," Johnson said. Not so for Atlanta, apparently. Only two nights earlier, the once-mighty Braves had watched Milwaukee's Ben Sheets whiff them 18 times, which made their futility against Johnson doubly frustrating.

The first batter, Jesse Garcia, tried to push a bunt toward first for a hit, but Shea Hillenbrand charged the ball and lunged to tag a headfirst-sliding Garcia for the first out. Johnson then struck out six of the next nine batters. Talk about being pale! "I felt my velocity got better as the game progressed," Johnson said. "My slider was the best it's ever been velocity wise. I threw a few split fingers; not many."

Perhaps the most crucial at-bat of the game came in the second, when Braves catcher Johnny Estrada, the only Atlanta player to see ball three all night (only seven others even got to ball two!), fouled off three straight 3-2 pitches before fanning. Estrada was the only Braves batter near the ball all night; he actually saw 22 pitches in three at-bats, nearly 20 percent of Johnson's total of 117. Finally, Estrada swung and missed and the march to perfection continued.

Johnson got all the offensive help he would need when Alex Cintron (who was all of 10 years old when Johnson made his MLB debut in 1988) doubled home Danny Bautista in the bottom of the second. (In the seventh, Cintron scored Arizona's second run on a Chad Tracy single.) Cintron ended up defusing the only possible Atlanta hit in the sixth when he threw out Mike Hampton after charging a bouncing ball on the grass at shortstop.

Things just got nasty after that. Johnson simply had his way with the Braves, who could neither figure out his slider nor catch up with his fastball, which was timed in excess of 97 mph more than half a dozen times that night.

As the mowing down moved on, Brenly, and all the Diamondbacks' players and staff, dove headlong into the superstition pool. "It wasn't foremost on my

> "A lot of people said, 'He's not going to be the pitcher he was.' Anybody that knows me knows I'll give everything I can to be the pitcher I've always been."
> —Randy Johnson

RANDY JOHNSON'S PERFECT GAME
MAY 18, 2004

Arizona	AB	R	H	RBI
Tracy, 3b	4	0	2	1
Kata, 2b	5	0	0	0
Gonzalez, lf	3	0	0	0
Hillenbrand, 1b	4	0	1	0
Finley, cf	4	0	1	0
Bautista, rf	4	1	1	0
Cintron, ss	4	1	3	1
Hammock, c	3	0	0	0
Johnson, p	4	0	0	0
Totals	**35**	**2**	**8**	**2**

Atlanta	AB	R	H	RBI
Garcia, ss	3	0	0	0
Franco, 1b	3	0	0	0
C. Jones, lf	3	0	0	0
A. Jones, cf	3	0	0	0
Estrada, c	3	0	0	0
Drew, rf	3	0	0	0
Derosa, 3b	3	0	0	0
Green, 2b	3	0	0	0
Hampton, p	2	0	0	0
Perez, ph	1	0	0	0
Totals	**27**	**0**	**0**	**0**

	1	2	3	4	5	6	7	8	9	R	H	E
Ari	0	1	0	0	0	0	1	0	0	2	8	0
Atl	0	0	0	0	0	0	0	0	0	0	0	3

Arizona	IP	H	R	ER	BB	K
Johnson (W)	9	0	0	0	0	13

Atlanta	IP	H	R	ER	BB	K
Hampton (L)	9	8	2	2	3	5

Time—2:13; Att.—23,381

CHAPTER 37

mind until after the sixth," Brenly said. "From that point on, everybody on the field, everybody in the dugout, was on pins and needles trying to make sure we sat in the same place, did the same things, and didn't do anything to disrupt the rhythm." Seated firmly on the bat rack the whole game, Brenly also tapped Matt Kata's bat with each Johnson windup.

Johnson and his young catcher, Robby Hammock, were playing the same tune all night, too. "The job Robby did back there was amazing," Johnson said. "I shook him off two or three times. That was in the eighth and ninth. It's nice when you're on the same page as your catcher." It's also nice when you wrote the book: Hammock called the shake offs "more like stare offs."

The ninth was played amid as much noise as 23,381 history witnessing fans at Turner Field could muster. Mark DeRosa led off and grounded easily to second. Young second baseman Nick Green made it an even dozen strikeouts. Pinch-hitting for Mike Hampton, who had allowed only two runs on eight hits for his best performance of a disappointing season, Eddie Perez thought he might have a chance to break things up. After all, the Atlanta backup catcher had six hits against Johnson in 13 career at-bats, including a homer and a pair of doubles. This night, however, he didn't have a prayer. Johnson mowed him down, with strike three hitting 98 on the gun, bringing Hammock racing to the mound and the Arizona team spilling out of the dugout.

Hammock got there first, quickly whipping off his mask and helmet so he wouldn't bruise Johnson's chest, since that's about how high he comes up to his towering pitcher. Johnson, for his part, pointed his glove at the sky, as he does after all wins, a gesture that speaks to his continuing relationship with his father's memory. He then was surrounded by the Diamondbacks, a tower of power looking down on a party.

Though certainly not subdued, Johnson's celebration was a far cry from David Cone's prayerful emotion. But that's how the big lefty is. He was even laid-back in the postgame news conference, calling the win for the team the big news.

"Obviously I knew what was going on," he said. "I've been in that situation before and I knew. That's a lesson for young pitchers: don't lose your focus." He also noted that he was especially happy for Hammock: "He was probably the most excited one out there."

"He's gotten better with age," said Atlanta's Chipper Jones after the game. "He's starting to use the outside part of the plate and has added a pitch over the last year or two." Johnson's ability to continue to improve can be traced to his phenomenal workout routine and his God's gift of a left arm. In fact, the 14 years (and 219 wins) between Johnson's two no-hitters (his first was with Seattle in 1990) were the most ever by a pitcher. The feat also made him the fifth pitcher to throw no-nos in each league. Jayson Stark of espn.com noted that only Johnson and Cy Young have thrown a perfect game "more than 200 wins deep into" a career. This was win number 234 for Johnson; it was Young's 381st.

More getting better with age? From the day he turned 40 to this game against Atlanta, Johnson started 12 games. Among them were a one-hitter, a two-hitter, and this perfect game.

"A lot of people said, 'He's not going to be the pitcher he was,'" Johnson told the *New York Daily News* late that evening. "Anybody that knows me knows I'll give everything I can to be the pitcher I've always been."

In the end, Johnson joined many of his teammates in the Ritz-Carlton bar in Atlanta late that night. The big man was buying and laughing it up with kids who were in T-ball when he was first firing bee-bees.

"You guys keep saying I'm old," he had told reporters earlier that evening. "And someday I will be." But not tonight, baby. Not tonight.

Top 10 from a guy Who's 6′10″

One of the bonuses that Cy Young, Addie Joss, and Don Larsen—heck, even Len Barker—could not enjoy was having one's perfect game celebrated on a late-night talk show. The day after his perfect game, Randy Johnson taped a spot for David Letterman in which the newly perfect lefty read the following top 10 list:

10. After this, I can go 0–15 for the rest of the year and honestly not give a crap.

9. My pregame dinner at Denny's? On the house!

8. Shows everyone that even though I'm 40, I can still . . . I'm sorry, I lost my train of thought.

7. Cool to get a congratulatory phone call from the president, even though he kept calling me "Larry."

6. Can walk up to the guys who've thrown no-hitters and whisper "loser."

5. All the pine tar I can eat!

4. Your catcher hugs you and it feels kinda . . . nice.

3. Maybe people will finally get over the time I killed that bird.

2. It's just one more thing about me that's perfect—am I right, ladies?

1. George Steinbrenner just offered me a billion dollars to sign with the Yankees.

Randy Johnson is mobbed by teammates after pitching a perfect game against the Atlanta Braves. At age 41, Johnson became the oldest player to pitch a perfect game.

CHAPTER 37

Closing Thoughts

Perhaps the greatest single change in modern baseball's first century was the emergence of the relief pitcher, or closer, as a vital component of any championship team—a thesis that is borne out statistically.

In 1903, the third year of the modern era, pitchers completed 85.6 percent of the games they started. Ten years later, they completed 53.4 percent. By 1953, the percentage of games completed was down to 34.8. And in 2003, only 4.3 percent of games were completed by the pitchers who started them.

Additionally, in modern baseball's first eight years, the major league record for saves was eight (although the save didn't become a statistic until 1969). That record jumped to 15 saves in 1924; 27 in 1949; 29 in 1961; 32 in 1966; 38 in 1973; 45 in 1983, to the current mark of 57 saves by Bobby Thigpen of the Chicago White Sox in 1990.

There was no such thing as a relief specialist in baseball's early days. That job usually fell to the "ace" of a pitching staff, called on to finish games on days he was not scheduled to start. Consequently, such fabled pitching names as Christy Mathewson, Mordecai "Three Finger" Brown, Carl Hubbell, and Dizzy Dean in the National League, and Chief Bender, "Big" Ed Walsh, Eddie Plank, Carl Mays, Bob Shawkey, Urban Shocker, "Sad" Sam Jones, and Lefty Grove in the American all led their leagues in saves.

Acknowledged as baseball's first pitcher to be used almost exclusively in relief was Washington's Fred "Firpo" Marberry, who got his nickname because he bore a strong facial resemblance to Argentine heavyweight Luis Firpo, who once knocked Jack Dempsey out of the ring. In a nine-year period from 1924 to 1932, Marberry led the American League in saves five times and raised the saves record twice, to 15 in 1924 and to 22 in 1926.

Soon after Marberry, the Yankees employed Wilcy Moore and Johnny Murphy as relief specialists, while most other teams adhered to the practice of using starting pitchers to finish up games. Bullpen specialists began to emerge after World War II—Ace Adams with the New York Giants, Hugh Casey with the Brooklyn Dodgers, Russ Christopher with the Cleveland Indians, Alpha Brazle and Ted Wilks with the St. Louis Cardinals, and Jim Konstanty with the Philadelphia Phillies. However,

pitchers like Allie Reynolds of the Yankees and Ellis Kinder of the Red Sox continued to perform double duty as both starters and relievers, pitching out of the bullpen to save games between starts.

At the time, being relegated to the bullpen was considered a demotion. Relief pitchers generally either were pitchers not deemed good enough to make the starting rotation, or aging veterans who no longer had the stuff or the stamina to go nine.

The first to gain national prominence and change the perception of the relief pitcher was the Yankees' Joe Page, a charismatic and flamboyant character who, when called out of the bullpen, would fling his warm-up jacket rakishly over his shoulder, vault over the bullpen fence, and march majestically to the mound to fire his blistering fastball past enemy batters. In 1949, Page raised the saves record to 27, and for years, was considered the prototype reliever, spawning a succession of hard-throwing relief pitchers like Dick "the Monster" Radatz, Don McMahon, Terry Forster, Goose Gossage, and Lee Smith.

It wasn't until the sixties that the relief pitcher blossomed as a bona fide star almost on equal footing with the starting pitcher. In a 13-year span from 1961 to 1973, the major league record for saves was broken six times, from Luis Arroyo's 29 in 1961 (tied by Dick Radatz in 1964), to Ted Abernathy's 31 in 1965, to Jack Aker's 32 in 1966, to Wayne Granger's 35 in 1970, to Clay Carroll's 37 in 1972, to John Hiller's 38 in 1973.

Hiller's record stood for 10 seasons until Dan Quisenberry saved 45 games for the Kansas City Royals in 1983, and the explosion of relief pitchers was on in earnest.

Through the years relief pitchers have consisted of one-year wonders like Turk Lown, Mike Fornieles, Minnie Rojas, Al Worthington, Bill Campbell, Hal Woodeschick, Dave Giusti, Steve Bedrosian, Jeff Russell, Mark Davis, Jeff Brantley, and Bobby Thigpen; pitchers with quirky, funky motions like Al "the Mad Hungarian" Hrabosky and sub-mariners Russ Christopher, Ted Abernathy, and Dan Quisenberry; or pitchers with trick pitches like Roy Face's forkball, Arroyo's and John Franco's screwball, Hoyt Wilhelm's and Barney Schultz' knuckleball, Bruce Sutter's split-finger fastball, Mariano Rivera's cutter, and Sparky Lyle's slider (Lyle once described his career as "16 years in the big leagues without ever throwing a fastball for a strike").

> At the time, being relegated to the bullpen was considered a demotion. Relief pitchers generally either were pitchers not deemed good enough to make the starting rotation, or aging veterans who no longer had the stuff or the stamina to go nine.

The great relief pitchers of the sixties and seventies—Lindy McDaniel, Sparky Lyle, Bruce Sutter, Mike Marshall—often were called upon when the game was on the line, in the eighth inning, seventh, even as early as the sixth, something that's frowned upon these days. Now a relief pitcher (they're called "closers" today) rarely comes into a game before the ninth, and usually to start the inning.

That practice had its origin with Tony LaRussa, manager of the Oakland Athletics in the late eighties and early nineties. With a lead, LaRussa would bring in a set-up man (Rick Honeycutt) to pitch the eighth inning, then a closer (Dennis Eckersley) to pitch the ninth. Eckersley, who had won 20 games as a starter for Boston in 1978, became the dominant closer of his time. In five years, from 1988 to 1992, he saved 220 games, twice leading the American League, with 45 saves in 1988 and 51 in 1992. In 130 $^{1}/_{3}$ innings over two seasons, 1988–1989, he walked just seven batters.

Eckersley would ride that success into the Baseball Hall of Fame, only the third player to enter the shrine primarily as a reliever. Hoyt Wilhelm was inducted in 1985. Rollie Fingers joined him in 1992, followed by Eck in 2004.

It could be the start of a trend. With three relievers now in Cooperstown, can Goose Gossage, Bruce Sutter, Lee Smith, Trevor Hoffman, John Smoltz, Mariano Rivera, and Eric Gagne be far behind?

Eckersley raised the bar for excellence by relief pitchers during the eighties and nineties and was rewarded with a ticket to Cooperstown.

CHAPTER 38

Page (center), about to be mobbed by fans and teammates after closing out the 1949 World Series at Ebbets Field, was the first relief pitcher to gain national prominence in that role.

Quisenberry's 45 saves in 1983 signaled the official dawn of the closer's era.

Top 20 Pitchers of All Time*

1. Sandy Koufax (50 points)

Yrs.	W	L	Pct.	ERA	CG	SHO	K
12	165	87	.655	2.76	137	40	2,396

2. Walter Johnson (46)

Yrs.	W	L	Pct.	ERA	CG	SHO	K
21	417	279	.599	2.17	531	110	3,509

3. Bob Feller (44)

Yrs.	W	L	Pct.	ERA	CG	SHO	K
18	266	162	.621	3.25	279	44	2,581

4. Warren Spahn (43)

Yrs.	W	L	Pct.	ERA	CG	SHO	K
21	363	245	.597	3.09	382	63	2,583

5. Lefty Grove (41)

Yrs.	W	L	Pct.	ERA	CG	SHO	K
17	300	141	.680	3.06	298	35	2,266

6. Bob Gibson (40)

Yrs.	W	L	Pct.	ERA	CG	SHO	K
17	251	174	.591	2.91	255	56	3,117

7. Christy Mathewson (38)

Yrs.	W	L	Pct.	ERA	CG	SHO	K
17	373	188	.665	2.13	434	79	2,502

8. Steve Carlton (36)

Yrs.	W	L	Pct.	ERA	CG	SHO	K
24	329	244	.574	3.22	254	55	4,136

9. Tom Seaver (35)

Yrs.	W	L	Pct.	ERA	CG	SHO	K
20	311	205	.603	2.86	231	61	3,640

10. Randy Johnson (34)**

Yrs.	W	L	Pct.	ERA	CG	SHO	K
16	230	114	.669	3.10	88	35	3,871

11. Grover Cleveland Alexander (34)

Yrs.	W	L	Pct.	ERA	CG	SHO	K
20	373	208	.642	2.56	437	90	2,198

12. Nolan Ryan (33)

Yrs.	W	L	Pct.	ERA	CG	SHO	K
27	324	292	.526	3.19	222	61	5,714

13. Roger Clemens (32)**

Yrs.	W	L	Pct.	ERA	CG	SHO	K
20	310	160	.660	3.19	117	46	4,099

14. Cy Young (27)

Yrs.	W	L	Pct.	ERA	CG	SHO	K
22	511	316	.618	2.63	749	76	2,803

15. Juan Marichal (25)

Yrs.	W	L	Pct.	ERA	CG	SHO	K
16	243	142	.631	2.89	244	52	2,303

16. Carl Hubbell (21)

Yrs.	W	L	Pct.	ERA	CG	SHO	K
16	253	154	.622	2.98	260	36	1,677

17. Robin Roberts (18)

Yrs.	W	L	Pct.	ERA	CG	SHO	K
19	286	245	.539	3.41	305	45	2,357

18. Jim Palmer (17)

Yrs.	W	L	Pct.	ERA	CG	SHO	K
19	268	152	.638	2.86	211	53	2,212

19. Greg Maddux (16)**

Yrs.	W	L	Pct.	ERA	CG	SHO	K
18	289	163	.639	2.89	103	34	2,765

20. Whitey Ford (14)

Yrs.	W	L	Pct.	ERA	CG	SHO	K
16	236	106	.690	2.75	156	45	1,956

* Consensus, point-driven list based on the submissions of the eight contributors (at right).

** Player is still active. Numbers are through the 2003 season.

Contributors

Ralph Kiner was one of baseball's preeminent sluggers of the postwar era, belting 369 home runs in an injury-shortened, 10-year Hall of Fame career from 1946 to 1955. He led the National League in homers a record seven straight seasons, including two 50-plus seasons and a then–National League record 101–home run, two-year output in 1949 and 1950. He has been broadcasting New York Mets games since the team's inception in 1962.

Ernie Harwell was the voice of the Detroit Tigers for 42 years before retiring from broadcasting following the 2002 season. Harwell's career spanned 55 years, and in 1981 he received the Ford C. Frick Award for broadcasting excellence from the National Baseball Hall of Fame.

Jim Kaat spent 25 years in the major leagues, retiring in 1983 after having played more seasons than any player in modern history to that point. He appeared in 898 games, pitched 4,528 innings, and won 283 games and 16 Gold Gloves. He later went into broadcasting and has been a television analyst for the New York Yankees since 1995.

Jerome Holtzman was one of the most widely read and respected baseball writers in the world before being named the official historian for Major League Baseball by Commissioner Allan H. "Bud" Selig in 1999. He began covering baseball in 1957 and worked the Cubs and White Sox beats for the *Chicago Sun-Times* and *Chicago Tribune* before becoming a national baseball writer and syndicated columnist.

Emil J. "Buzzie" Bavasi spent almost 50 years in baseball, starting out as an office boy for the Brooklyn Dodgers in 1939. He rose to become executive vice president and general manager of the Dodgers, in Brooklyn and Los Angeles, was president of the San Diego Padres, and executive vice president of the California Angels until he retired in 1985. He still follows the game closely.

Joe Garagiola joined his hometown St. Louis Cardinals as a catcher in 1946 after service in World War II and ended a nine-year playing career with a .258 batting average for the Cards, Pirates, Cubs, and New York Giants. He then embarked on a very successful broadcasting career and, in 1991, was inducted into the Broadcaster's Wing of the National Baseball Hall of Fame.

Phil Pepe has authored more than 35 sports books, including collaborations with Mickey Mantle and Whitey Ford. He was the Yankees beat writer for the *New York Daily News* for 14 seasons and is a past president of the Baseball Writers Association of America.

James Buckley Jr. has written more than 25 sports books, including *Perfect: The Inside Story of Baseball's 16 Perfect Games*. He is the owner and editorial director of Shoreline Publishing Group, a book packaging and editorial services company in Santa Barbara, California.

Index

Numbers in *italics* represent photographs.